PENGUIN BOOKS

BBC BOOKS

A GUIDE TO PARLIAMENT

David Michael Davis was born in 1948 and was educated at Warwick University, London Business School and Harvard University. After various appointments with Tate and Lyle plc he was made a Director in 1987, and was elected as Member of Parliament for Boothferry in the same year. In November 1990 he was appointed Assistant Government Whip. Before that he was Parliamentary Private Secretary to the Hon. Francis Maude MP and is a past member of the National Union Executive Committee and the NUEC General Purposes Committee. Mr Davis was also the National Chairman of the Federation of Conservative Students. He founded the Newham sixth-form Scholarship Scheme in 1982, was the originator of the Tate and Lyle/Touche Ross Student Innovation Awards in 1985 and was an executive member of the Industrial Society in 1985. He was Parliamentary Secretary at the Office of Public Service and Science from May 1993 until July 1994, when he was appointed Minister of State at the Foreign and Common-wealth Office. He was made a Privy Councillor in the 1997 New Year's Honours List and was elected as Member of Parliament for Haltemprice and Howden in the same year.

David Davis has written various articles and pamphlets, including one on the National Health Service and one entitled 'Clear the Decks', discussing the abolition of the National Dock Labour Scheme. His first book was *How to Turn Round a Company*. His special interests include industrial and trade policy, industrial relations, law and order, the NHS and social services.

David Davis is married to Doreen and they have three children. His hobbies include mountaineering, skiing and flying light aircraft.

DAVID DAVIS, MP

A Guide to Parliament

PENGUIN BOOKS
BBC BOOKS

PENGUIN BOOKS

BBC BOOKS

Published by the Penguin Group and BBC Worldwide Ltd
Penguin Books Ltd, 27 Wrights Lane, London w 8 5 tz, England
Penguin Putnam Inc., 375 Hudson Street, New York, New York 10014, USA
Penguin Books Australia Ltd, Ringwood, Victoria, Australia
Penguin Books Canada Ltd, 10 Alcorn Avenue, Toronto, Ontario, Canada m 4 v 3 b 2
Penguin Books (NZ) Ltd, 182–190 Wairau Road, Auckland 10, New Zealand

Penguin Books Ltd, Registered Offices: Harmondsworth, Middlesex, England

First published by BBC Books, a division of BBC Worldwide Limited, 1989
Published, with revisions, in Penguin Books 1997

3 5 7 9 10 8 6 4 2

Copyright © David Davis, 1989, 1997

BBC ™ BBC used under licence

Set in 10/13 pt Monotype Garamond
Typeset by Rowland Phototypesetting Ltd,
Bury St Edmunds, Suffolk
Printed in England by Clays Ltd, St Ives plc

To all unsung heroes of the Palace of Westminster –
the clerks, the badge messengers, the policemen and
all the other staff who make old institutions work as
smoothly as a well-oiled machine

CONTENTS

INTRODUCTION

'Every politician is emphatically a promising politician.'
G. K. Chesterton, *The Red Moon of Meru*

New Members of Parliament (MPs), if they are anything like the author, approach their first time in the House of Commons with some trepidation. The chamber itself is awe-inspiring. It is the place, albeit rebuilt, where great men have crafted history, and where the map of the modern world was largely drawn up. Churchill and Chamberlain, Baldwin and Balfour, Palmerston and Parnell – all spoke here. Anyone who approaches with anything other than humility is heading for a fall.

The sense of history does not just infect the building, however. It also dictates how the House is run. Over hundreds of years there has grown up an enormous body of rules that govern the procedures of the House. These are laid down in a book called Erskine May (Sir Erskine May's *Treatise on the Law, Privileges, Proceedings and Usage of Parliament*, 1844) – a 'Bible' that ran to 1,079 pages in its twenty-first edition. Accordingly, it is not surprising that even MPs of many years' standing trip up occasionally on the rules of the House.

To new Members the system is barely intelligible. Most of us spent our first year learning from our mistakes. This is not to say that the system is in any way unnecessary or wrong. Every rule has its reason, but, with such accumulated complexity, it would not be surprising if it seemed like mindless mummery to an outsider.

This book therefore describes what MPs are attempting to do in the House. Are they trying to get reform of a bill or publicity for an injustice? Are they really fascinated by the matter under debate, or are they simply trying to deny time to subsequent business? Is the point of order really a point of order, or is the MP just drawing attention to something or even creating disorder? With this perspective, avid watchers of the proceedings of the House might well find themselves changing their opinions about some of the members. They may, for example, disapprove of the politics of Dennis Skinner or Bill Cash; but they will probably acquire a grudging admiration for the skilful way that they manipulate the procedures – precisely as they are intended to be used – to propagate the rights of back-benchers and their constituents against power of Government. Another of the great pleasures of Parliament may also become apparent: that, amidst the serious business and dignified function, there is invariably a vein of humour and self-mockery running just below the surface.

Broadcasting of debates began on radio in April 1978, and televised coverage of debates in the House of Lords began in January 1985. On 21 November 1989, as an experiment, the House of Commons televised its first debate. The experiment, extended after a year, has by now become the norm.

Television has changed the proceedings of the House of Commons for ever. Whether these changes are ultimately for the best will be decided in years to come, but looking back on the first seven years, it is possible to measure the success of televised debating and suggest areas of improvement. Proceedings for the first time have become accessible to millions. With this has come increased public knowledge of current events and scrutiny of our elected officials. Both the positive and the negative effects of our parliamentary democracy have been highlighted. (Some of these were covered in the Jopling Committee Report and a number of measures were proposed to improve the operation of the House: see page 164.) Overall, with the increasing visibility of MPs and greater public knowledge of current debates have come sharper scrutiny of MPs and increased responsibilities.

The procedures of the Houses of Parliament are not, in themselves, very exciting. This book attempts to leaven the subject with amusing anecdotes, quotations and pieces of history. Nevertheless, the subject itself is deadly serious in one respect. Parliamentary procedure is a fundamental part of the unwritten constitution that has given Britain its liberties, tolerance and relative freedom from extremism in Government. It is the gift to our generation from previous parliamentarians, and is a gift well worth preserving. Enjoy your politician-watching – and remember the following:

'You can fool all the people some of the time, and some of the people all of the time, but you cannot fool all the people all of the time.' *Abraham Lincoln*, 1858

'You can't fool all the people all of the time, but do it once and it lasts five years.' *Eric Forth*, MP

ACKNOWLEDGEMENTS

Politics can be described as the art of competitive plagiarism. This book is no exception. Much of the material in it has come from the insights and anecdotes of many Members of Parliament with far longer experience than the author. So many of them have been so generous in sharing their knowledge that it would be impossible to mention them all here. I hope they will accept my apologies and gratitude and forgive the unaccustomed anonymity that has befallen them. Some of them have themselves gone into print, and I am particularly grateful to Gerald Kaufman, Austin Mitchell, Peter Hennessy and Richard Needham for permission to use extracts from their books, and to Robert Rhodes James, historian, author and past Clerk of the House, for his sage advice on the text.

Comments, wisecracks and stories from numerous lobby correspondents and sketchwriters have helped make this book more readable. Again, there are too many to list, but Simon Heffer, Matthew Parris and Philip Webster have all made substantive suggestions which have found their way into the text. Professor Philip Norton, in giving advice, deployed his formidable knowledge of both the theory and the practicalities of Parliament. To him and to Simon Burns MP and to Alan Sandall I am indebted for their encyclopedic knowledge and remarkable insights.

I am also grateful to Mrs Pat Mitchell of Queen Margaret's School, Escrick, and Miss Carol Henderson of Goole Grammar School, who both gave generously of their advice from a classroom perspective. Similarly I would like to thank my own daughter, Rebecca, who provided the view from the other side of the desk – that of an intelligent fourteen-year-old checking that this work did not too easily slip into tedium. Fortunately she acquitted me of that charge.

Finally, my thanks to Fiona Barron, Conor McGrath and Eric Aaronson, all of whom gave generously of their time on the 'treadmill' that is an inevitable part of the process of creating any book. I know of few people who would so willingly have put in such long hours of hard work for such a tough taskmaster; without them it could not have been done.

I

GRAND OCCASIONS

THE STATE OPENING OF PARLIAMENT

Of all the great occasions that surround parliamentary procedure, the most colourful ceremony of all is the State Opening of Parliament. This occurs once a year, at the beginning of each parliamentary session, when the monarch travels from Buckingham Palace to the Palace of Westminster to deliver the annual address to both Houses of Parliament – that is, to the House of Commons and to the House of Lords. There is much pomp and circumstance – but not necessarily an excess of pomposity. In his soft Welsh accent and with a wicked gleam in his eye, John Stradling Thomas once described how he took part in this procession when he was Treasurer of Her Majesty's Household (the smart name for Government Deputy Chief Whip). According to Simon Hoggart, who related the incident in *Punch*,

He and Spencer le Marchant [another Government Whip] were bowling along in an open carriage waving to the crowds with their white sticks when John spotted an attractive young lady journalist he knew, so he blew her a kiss! Her surprised look was to be expected since Labour MPs never did anything like that as they were too serious – sitting up straight like sergeant-majors – which, quite possibly, half of them were. Not like the Tory ministers – half of them regard royalty as their social inferiors!

The State Opening is a colourful event. Peers wear their scarlet and ermine robes, and the procession down the Royal Gallery towards the House of Lords is lined by Beefeaters. Wearing her parliamentary robes and the Imperial State Crown, the Queen proceeds from the Robing Room to the chamber of the House of Lords to deliver the Queen's Speech. This speech has, in fact, been written by the Government and outlines the Government's programme for the coming session.

PROCEDURE

When the Queen has taken her place on the throne in the House of Lords, Black Rod, an officer of the House of Lords, is sent to summon the Members of the House of Commons to the chamber of the Lords. Just before Black Rod arrives at the Commons, the door is slammed in his face. He must then knock three times to enter. He is then admitted. This bizarre ritual is performed to remind the House that the monarch may under no circumstances enter the debating chamber of the House of Commons. When you sit in the Strangers' Gallery or walk on a tour of the debating chamber, consider that you are some-where where the Queen may not go. This dates back to 1642, when King Charles I burst into the debating chamber of the House of Commons and demanded that the House present to him the five Members of Parliament who had 'treasonably' spoken against him, so he could have them arrested. The five Members, having learned of the King's intention, had fled down the Thames moments before, and the Speaker of the House of Commons at the time, Lenthall, asserted the authority of Parliament over the monarchy, replying, 'May it please Your Majesty, I have neither eyes to see, nor tongue to speak in this place, but as the House is pleased to direct me, whose servant I am here, and I humbly beg Your Majesty's pardon that I cannot give any other answer than this to what Your Majesty is pleased to demand of me.'

Black Rod is then admitted as far as the Bar of the House, from where he proclaims, 'Madam Speaker, the Queen commands this Honourable House to attend Her Majesty immediately in the House of Peers.' The Members proceed two by two to the Lords, led by the Speaker. When as many as possible have fitted into the chamber, the Lord Chancellor hands the Queen a copy of the speech.

Once the Queen has delivered the speech, the royal procession leaves the chamber. The Members of the Commons then return to their chamber and the Speaker directs that 'the Gracious speech from the Throne to both Houses of Parliament be printed at the appropriate place in the Votes and Proceedings'.

Extract from the Queen's Speech, November 1994

My Lords and Members of the House of Commons

The Duke of Edinburgh and I look forward to receiving the State Visit of His Highness the Amir of Kuwait in May and His Excellency the President of Finland in October next year.

The Duke of Edinburgh and I look forward to our State Visit to South Africa in March. We also look forward to our visit to New Zealand and to the Commonwealth Heads of Government Meeting there in November next year.

My Government attach the highest importance to national security. They will work to continue the process of NATO's adaptation to the changing security environment to allow it to play a wider role in protecting stability throughout Europe. At the Budapest summit in December they will seek to enhance the role of the Conference on Security and Co-operation in Europe in conflict prevention and resolution. They will also work for full implementation of the Conventional Armed Forces in Europe Treaty. The United Kingdom's nuclear deterrent will be maintained.

My Government will continue its efforts to promote a peaceful settlement in the former Yugoslavia . . .

My Government will play an active part in tackling drug misuse, drug trafficking and organized crime at home and abroad.

Support for consolidation of a peaceful and stable democracy in South Africa will remain a priority.

My Government will continue to work for the long-term stability and prosperity of Hong Kong. They will seek to develop co-operation with China to implement the Sino-British Joint Declaration in the best interests of the Hong Kong people and a smooth transition in 1997.

Support for political and economic reform in the former Communist countries of Europe and Asia will continue.

My Government will maintain support for the Middle East Peace Process.

They will work for yet stronger ties with the countries of the Asia Pacific region.

Members of the House of Commons

Estimates for the public service will be laid before you.

My Lords and Members of the House of Commons

Legislation will be introduced to give force to the changes in the European Community's system of own resources following the agreement at the Edinburgh European Council.

My Government will continue with firm financial policies designed to support continuing economic growth and rising employment, based on permanently low inflation.

Fiscal policy will continue to be set to bring the budget deficit back towards balance over the medium term. My Government will reduce the share of national income taken by the public sector.

My Government will continue to promote enterprise, to improve the working of the labour market, and to strengthen the supply performance of the economy. They will bring forward legislation to promote increased competition in the gas industry and to reform the agricultural tenancy laws in England and Wales. A Bill will be introduced to create a Jobseeker's Allowance, reforming benefits for unemployed people and giving them better help into work.

Legislation will be introduced to equalize the State pension age between men and women and to improve security, equality and choice in non-state pensions.

My Government will continue to implement policies and programmes responsive to the needs of the individual citizen, in line with the principles of the Citizen's Charter.

They will introduce a Bill to tackle discrimination against disabled people.

My Government will bring forward legislation to make further improvements to the management of the National Health Service; and to provide for people with a serious mental disorder discharged from hospital to be cared for under supervision.

Legislation will be introduced to transfer the Crown Agents and the commercial activities of the Atomic Energy Authority to the private sector; and to authorize the construction and operation by the private sector of a high speed rail link between London and the Channel Tunnel.

The delivery of environment policies will be strengthened by legislation to establish environment agencies for England and Wales, and for Scotland.

Legislation will be introduced to reform the Scottish Criminal Justice system.

In Northern Ireland my Government will build on the progress already made to secure peace and a comprehensive political accommodation founded on the principles of democracy and consent. They will uphold law and order and strive to strengthen the economy and create equality of opportunity for all sections of the community. They will seek to maintain close and constructive relations with the Republic of Ireland.

My Government will promote further measures of law reform.

Other measures will be laid before you.

My Lords and Members of the House of Commons

I pray that the blessing of Almighty God may rest upon your counsels.

THE COMMONS DEBATE

The debate on the Queen's Speech lasts six days in the Commons and four in the Lords. The motion in the Commons is proposed by two Members chosen by the Prime Minister. The debate includes contributions from all the party leaders, over half the Cabinet, many shadow spokesmen and women and a considerable number of back-benchers. At 10 p.m. on the sixth day of debate, the Speaker puts the question, the division bells start to ring out and the first vote of the new session takes place. This vote is, in essence, a statement of support – or opposition – to the principles of the Government's programme for the session.

On the day of the Queen's Speech, an interesting event that is often forgotten takes place: when the Members of the Commons return to their own chamber they do not immediately begin to debate the speech; instead, the Outlawries Bill, which is, unusually, not presented by any Member, is read. This bill is not intended to progress any further but it does have considerable constitutional importance. A similar bill – the Select Vestries Bill – is read in the House of Lords.

OUTLAWRIES BILL

The significance of the Outlawries Bill is that its reading reaffirms the right of the Commons to discuss a matter of their choice rather than having to turn immediately to the content of the monarch's address.

In 1676 Sir Thomas Lee explained the reasoning behind it:

[I] care not how soon the King's Speech is taken into consideration but would not lose the method and order of Parliament. You always begin with reading a Bill. The King's Speech is usually about Supply and that ought to be the last thing considered here.*

Also in 1676 Sir Thomas Meres defended the Commons' right to debate a topic of their choosing before the monarch's address: 'Though forms seem but little things, yet they are of great consequence.'

The practice of introducing a bill before considering other business dates back to at least 1558, and in 1604 a resolution was adopted 'that the first day of sitting in every Parliament, some one bill and no more receiveth a First Reading for form sake'. Until 1727 the bills were genuine proposals and many progressed further in the legislative process. In that year, however, this practice was changed and a bill with the present title was introduced. Ever since then, apart from 1741 and 1742, the Commons have given an Outlawries Bill its first reading before deliberating upon the King or Queen's Speech.

THE ELECTION OF THE SPEAKER

'The office of Speaker does not demand rare qualities. It demands common qualities in rare degree.' *Speaker Lowther*

The chairman or woman of the House of Commons is known as the Speaker, and is chosen from among the MPs themselves. A Speaker is traditionally elected at the beginning of a new Parliament, or when the previous Speaker ceases to be a Member (death or otherwise). This

* From public information fact sheet about the Outlawries Bill.

is because the House cannot conduct any business without a Speaker (except for this election). 'The Speaker', or Mr or Madam Speaker as he or she is always referred to in the House, is a title taken from a time when the main function was to act as spokesman or woman of the House to the sovereign.

PROCEDURE

The election takes place in the afternoon of the very first day of the new Parliament. It is the first ceremony newly elected MPs attend and is the first time they enter the chamber as a Member of Parliament. For this ceremony, the chamber is presided over by the Father of the House, the longest-serving Member. The current Father of the House is the Rt Hon. Sir Edward Heath, MP, who became an MP on 2 March 1950.

The presiding Member does not sit in the Speaker's chair, but at the clerks' table in front of the chair. Unless the retiring Speaker is presiding over the election of his or her successor, the mace is placed below, rather than above, the clerks' table and remains there until the Speaker-elect takes the chair. The mace, which is a symbol of Crown and Parliament, sits in the chamber during all sessions.

The formal election of the Speaker is usually preceded by inter-party consultations in order to agree on the most suitable Member to occupy the chair. He or she is usually an experienced MP, someone who is capable of giving impartial judgements and has the respect of all Members. Traditionally, Speakers are back-benchers who have not been ministers, but there have been occasions when the Speaker has had previous ministerial experience. In the past, Speakers were Members of the Government party when first elected to the chair, but Betty Boothroyd, the current Speaker, was a member of the main Opposition party when elected. Modern practice may now be for the Speakership to alternate between the two major parties.

The election of the Speaker starts promptly at 2.30 p.m. Once the Father of the House has taken his seat at the table, Black Rod arrives. As with the Queen's Speech, he must knock three times before entering.

On gaining admission he informs the Commons that 'the Lord Commissioners desire their immediate attendance ... to hear the commission read'. The Clerk and Members of the House of Commons then go to the Lords, where three gentlemen wearing tricorn hats order them to elect a Speaker. They then return to the Commons.

If more than one Member is nominated as Speaker, as happened with Betty Boothroyd, then the question is proposed for the first candidate and debated. The second candidate is put forward in the form of an amendment to the main question, with another proposer and seconder being called to speak. In fact, this has occurred only three times this century. In a division on 27 April 1992, by 372 votes to 238, Miss Boothroyd was elected as Speaker. Her appointment stands out for a number of other reasons: she was the first to be chosen from the Opposition benches this century, she was only the third to be chosen from Labour Party ranks and she was the first woman ever to be chosen by the House as its Speaker.

The candidates sit in the chamber among their fellow MPs, listening to the proposing and seconding speeches. The Member who has been proposed then makes a speech submitting himself or herself to the House. If there is more than one candidate, each will speak. There will then be a vote, and the Members who have been proposed give their votes to each other. Generally, however, a vote is avoided and Speakers are elected by their fellow MPs without opposition.

When the new Speaker has been elected, he or she rises from the back benches and is conducted to the chair by his or her proposer and seconder. Traditionally, Speakers-elect display some reluctance at this point, pretending that they do not want to be Speaker, and are dragged to the chair. This is a reminder of the time when no one wanted this job, since it had led to the death of several Speakers when they had conveyed unwelcome news to the sovereign – at a time when the monarch exercised real political power. It is believed that the first Speaker to show such reluctance was Sir Richard Waldegrave in 1381.

When they arrive at the chair, Speakers-elect stand on the top step and pause beside the chair for a moment as if to give the House a chance to change its mind. They then express their thanks for the honour that the House has bestowed upon them and take their seat. After the Speaker-elect has been congratulated by the Prime Minister, the Leader of the Opposition and other leading Members, the House adjourns.

The following day, after the Speaker-elect has taken the chair, Black Rod once again summons the Commons to the House of Lords. The Commons then attend the Lords. On this occasion the Speaker traditionally wore a small wig, court dress and no gown. Betty Boothroyd has chosen not to wear the usual full-bottomed wig favoured by her predecessors. In fact, she is the first in some time to hold the position with a full head of hair! From the Bar of the House of Lords, the Speaker-elect announces 'that in obedience to Her Majesty's command, Her Majesty's most faithful Commons have, in the exercise of their undoubted right and privileges, proceeded to the election of a Speaker'. He or she asks for the royal approval of the choice of Speaker. This is given by the Lord Chancellor, on behalf of the Queen, who announces 'that Her Majesty most readily approves and confirms —— as the Speaker'. It is believed that the royal approval has been refused only once, in 1678.

If it is a new Parliament, on behalf of the Commons the Speaker demands their 'ancient privileges' – that is, their right to speak freely. This again is another reminder of history:

By humble petition to Her Majesty, to all their ancient and undoubted rights and privileges, especially to freedom of speech in debate, to freedom from arrest and to free access to Her Majesty whenever occasion shall require.

Shortly afterwards everyone returns to the Commons. The Speaker goes to the chair and puts on his or her full gown, and the mace is placed on the table. The Speaker then takes the oath, followed by the Government front bench, then the Opposition and finally the remaining honourable Members.

If, during a Parliament, Speakers indicate that they wish to relinquish office, they continue to take the chair and perform their duties as Speaker until a new election is held, over which they preside.

THE QUALITIES OF THE SPEAKER

Once elected, the new Speaker will renounce party allegiance and become genuinely independent. The tradition of impartiality in the Speakership is very strong. It began with Arthur Onslow, who was Speaker for thirty-three years from 1728. This impartiality is demonstrated in the fact that Speakers do not usually vote, although they do retain a casting vote when there is a tie. The Speaker's casting vote was used seven times during the 1974–9 Parliament after the Government lost its majority.

Speakers are also barred from making speeches. They must be scrupulously impartial in their behaviour and ensure that the rights, privileges and dignities of the House are maintained. Speakers have complete control of procedures in the House and therefore have great prestige and respect. They have the power to discipline rebellious or difficult Members by 'naming' them and then it is up to the House to order their suspension. They must also have great skill and authority in responding to the moods of the House. They decide who will speak next within the chamber, calling Members by name rather than by constituency.

THE MAIDEN SPEECH

The first hurdle for a newly elected MP is the maiden speech. Making this first speech in the House of Commons is probably one of the most unforgettable events in the life of all MPs. Or it may be the event they most want to forget. Sir Winston Churchill described his maiden speech, in February 1901, as 'a terrible, thrilling, yet delicious, experience'.

Harold Macmillan, in his autobiography, compared making his maiden speech to his experiences in the war:

Except for 'going over the top' in war, there is hardly any experience so alarming as this ... There is a long period of waiting, when nerves are wrought up to a high pitch . . . Through the kindness of the Whips and the Speaker, it is usually arranged for a young Member to be informed at what time he is likely to be called; yet when this moment actually arrives there is a sense of dazed confusion. You stand up with a dozen or more other Members. The Speaker calls out a name. You can hardly distinguish whether it is yours. You hesitate, not knowing what to do. But as everybody else sits down, you conclude you must now go on.

Perhaps you have written out the text of the speech, in which case you read it clumsily and in breach of the strict traditions of the House. Or you try to memorize it, in which case you probably forget it completely . . . The furniture of the House is so arranged that when you stand up to speak the bench in front of you seems to catch you just below the knee and gives you the impression that you are about to fall headlong over. However, if you survive all these difficulties you can make a start.

The event is probably made slightly less traumatic by one of the traditions of the House – that a maiden speech will not be interrupted by other Members.

Most new MPs give their maiden in their first months in Parliament. In fact, of 125 new Members in June 1987, for example, about eighty had made their maiden speech by the end of July. Most Members try to get it out of the way as soon as possible, although there is actually no need to do so. And some opt to wait a bit longer. For Lord Maenan (1854–1951), the oldest peer to make a maiden speech, it was at age ninety-four years and 123 days in 1948. It is possible also to wait too long, as was the case for J. M. Richardson (Brigg), whose maiden speech of 5 May 1895 was also his last.

The length of the maiden and the style in which it is made vary, but most MPs conform to a pattern in a speech usually lasting about ten minutes. It begins with a few nice words about the previous Member, a description of the constituency, an indication of the Member's own parliamentary interests, and concludes with a short reference to the subject under debate. The tradition used to be that a maiden speech would not be controversial, but this has now changed to a certain extent.

Margaret Thatcher's maiden speech, which lasted thirty minutes, introduced a Private Member's Bill giving the press the right to attend and report council meetings. Benjamin Disraeli took three hours for his and was shouted down. Nicholas Fairbairn plunged straight into controversy in his maiden, as did A. P. Herbert, whose speech was described by Sir Winston Churchill as 'that was no maiden, that was a brazen hussy of a speech'. Stuart Holland began his maiden with a joke – 'accustomed as I am to public speaking' – but most are fairly serious.

A maiden speech can, of course, give a false impression of the new Member. A prime example of how first impressions in the House of Commons can be misleading is Benjamin Disraeli's maiden, on 7 December 1837. He spoke in a debate on Irish election petitions and was howled down. He gave way, but said that the time would come when Members would hear him. This heckling may have been the reason for his poor speech, but, even so, it proves how a successful career can develop from a disappointing debut.

By contrast, on 22 April 1969 Bernadette Devlin gave an excellent and most memorable maiden speech. She spoke on her very first day in the Commons, making an attack on Harold Wilson's policy on Northern Ireland. At the age of only twenty-one she surprised the House with her strong words, and Jeremy Thorpe, the Liberal leader at the time, spoke after her, describing her speech as an example of political courage. Nevertheless, this strong entrance to the House of Commons was perhaps misleading, as Ms Devlin's political career since then has been entirely unremarkable.

The next Member to speak after a maiden speech begins with formal praise of the new Member, however little deserved. Sir Edward Heath remarked after Robert Rhodes James's long maiden of twenty-three minutes, 'Congratulations on *both* your maiden speeches!'

Despite the common pattern, maiden speeches are always watched and listened to by the Members, because the House has a tradition of welcoming its new recruits in a gentlemanly manner – however much the newcomers may resent the ritual.

THE BUDGET STATEMENT

The Budget Statement is another grand annual occasion in the parliamentary year. The statement is delivered by the Chancellor of the Exchequer, usually on a Tuesday in November. (This is a recent return to an older tradition. In his five years as Chancellor of the Exchequer, Denis Healey delivered no less than fifteen 'budgets' or 'mini-budgets' – one every four months on average. This reflected the economic crisis of the 1970s. An annual Budget is now considered quite sufficient!)

The word 'budget' comes from the French *bougette*, meaning a 'small bag', and is thought to derive from a cartoon in a pamphlet of 1733 which showed Sir Robert Walpole (the Prime Minister and Chancellor) opening a bag (or budget) full of medicines and potions. Over the years, the Budget Statement has become the subject of intense media interest. Chancellors are photographed on the doorstep of their official residence, 11 Downing Street, holding a battered red dispatch box, which was first used to carry the Budget Speech to the House by William Gladstone around 1860. When the Chancellor rises after Question Time to deliver the speech, the House of Commons will be packed full of excited Members and the galleries will be similarly full of journalists and members of the public. The speech is broadcast live on both television and radio.

In the Budget Statement, the Chancellor discusses Britain's general economic situation and then goes on to explain the measures being proposed in order to raise the income required. The Budget Speech is a fairly detailed economic and financial statement of great national importance, and as such it is usually quite lengthy. The shortest Budget Speech was delivered in forty-five minutes by Benjamin Disraeli in 1867, but the longest ever, in 1853, took William Gladstone almost five hours to deliver! Because of its length, the Chancellor may drink alcohol when delivering the Budget Speech – currently the only occasion on which alcohol is allowed in the chamber. In the last century, Members are recorded as having been 'fortified' by spirits during particularly long-winded speeches, and Budget Statements are the last remnants of those more 'spirited' days.

The Chancellor's Sustenance

Different Chancellors have shown a wide range of tastes in drink to sustain them while giving their Budget Speech.

Hugh Dalton: *milk and rum*
As the only Chancellor to resign before the budget debate was over, he probably needed the rum

Sir Stafford Cripps: *an austere orange juice*
It is not recorded whether it was National Health orange juice

Hugh Gaitskell: *orange juice with a dash of rum*
Well, better than just orange juice

Rab Butler: *water*
Some of his Budgets were boring too

Harold Macmillan: *water*
You wouldn't think rationing had gone

Peter Thorneycroft: *water*
Not known as 'Mr Misery' for nothing

Derick Heathcoat Amory: *milk and honey with rum*
The milk and honey was presumably symbolic. It was not the rum that made him the only Chancellor to collapse while delivering the Budget Statement – that was overwork

Selwyn Lloyd: *whisky and water*
Well, he did introduce a tax on soft drinks!

Reginald Maudling: *unknown*
Like so much about Reggie

James Callaghan: *quinine and water*
He was about to be attacked by more than mosquitoes

Roy Jenkins: *unknown*
Probably claret, what else?

Anthony Barber: *water*
Yes, he zero-rated soft drinks for VAT!

Denis Healey: *brandy and water*
Brandy is used to resuscitate; the economy needed it more than him

Sir Geoffrey Howe: *gin and tonic*
His constituency is in the stockbroker belt

Nigel Lawson: *spritzer*
It became the yuppies' favourite drink

Kenneth Clarke: *Glenfarclas malt whisky*

Tremendous secrecy surrounds the drafting of the Budget Speech. Thus, in 1947 Chancellor Hugh Dalton had to resign after disclosing to a journalist one detail just minutes before he was due to deliver his speech to the House.

Chancellors receive advice from the Treasury's Budget Committee, which is composed of some of the most senior Treasury civil servants. They also consult the Prime Minister, and perhaps some senior Cabinet colleagues, but the full Budget Speech is revealed to the entire Cabinet only a few days before it is presented to Parliament.

THE BUDGET DEBATE

By tradition, the Budget Statement is not interrupted; in reality Hugh Dalton, Stafford Cripps, Hugh Gaitskell, Reginald Maudling, James Callaghan and Nigel Lawson have all given way to questions, interruptions and general barracking.

In 1988 the interruptions were so rowdy that the Speaker reprimanded Alex Salmond, the Scottish Nationalist MP for Banff and Buchan, by 'naming' him and then suspended the debate. In 1989 attempts were made by the Celtic Nationalist parties to pre-empt the entire Budget Speech (see page 52). It was feared that such behaviour, which is encouraged by the knowledge that the eyes of the country are on the House on Budget Day, would not augur well for televised Budgets, but in fact they have passed off without incident.

When the Chancellor finishes his speech, the Leader of the Opposition replies to it. The Budget is then debated on the floor of the House for four or five days. After this, the House votes on a series of Ways and Means resolutions, which deal with the taxation elements of the Budget. When these have all been voted upon, the Finance Bill is introduced. The Finance Bill embodies all the Budget proposals, and takes about three months to pass through the legislative process of both Houses. The Bill has to receive its second reading, which normally lasts for only one day, no more than twenty sitting days after the end of the Budget debate.

Until 1968 the committee stage of the Finance Bill had been taken on the floor of the House; it is now dealt with by a standing committee. This committee examines the technical clauses of the bill, but the more controversial and novel aspects of the bill are still taken by a committee of the whole House.

THE FINANCE BILL

Since they are so central to a government's programme, Budgets and their ensuing Finance Bills are invariably controversial, no matter how dull their content. In 1976 this controversy went beyond normal party lines and became a virtual constitutional battle. Generally, control over taxation is the sole right of the Commons. An attempt by the Lords to amend the Finance Bill would be seen as an infringement of Commons privilege (see page 95). In 1976 the Government was accused of 'tacking' non-tax legislation on to a tax bill. The disputed legislation gave powers to the Inland Revenue to break into premises and seek evidence of tax fraud. Some Members of the House of Lords objected, and there ensued a sizeable battle in the Commons.

In one of the better spoofs in recent parliamentary history, Nicholas Ridley put down a series of amendments to the bill giving taxpayers the right to break into a tax office when they had reason to believe there was evidence entitling them to tax refunds. These amendments were rejected for being 'tendered in a spirit of mockery'.

A great many more serious amendments are proposed to the Finance

Bill – 300–400 in fact – but not all of these are debated. A number of changes will be made to the bill as it passes through the Commons, because no Government will cut short debate on the Finance Bill except as a last resort. The Government will therefore accept some changes in order to save parliamentary time. The bill then receives its report stage and third reading in the Commons, and passes to the House of Lords for consideration. A Finance Bill cannot be amended by the Lords, because of the supremacy of the Commons so far as the making of financial legislation is concerned, and so it normally passes through the Lords in one day. The bill then goes for Royal Assent, which it must receive by 5 May. On receipt of the Royal Assent a bill becomes an act, and is described by the year in which it received such assent: thus the Finance Bill becomes Finance Act 1995, for example.

While it is the Finance Act that gives final legal authority to all the Budget proposals, many of the proposals relating to taxation come into effect within hours of the conclusions of the Chancellor's speech. This is necessary to avoid stockpiling. If the Chancellor were to announce that the tax on cigarettes, for example, was to go up, then, unless this proposal could be immediately enacted, smokers would buy a supply of cigarettes in order to avoid the rise in prices that would result when the Finance Act came into force.

THE PROVISIONAL COLLECTION OF TAXES ACT

The Provisional Collection of Taxes Act 1968, which is a re-enactment of a 1913 act of the same name, allows changes and continuations of existing taxes proposed in the Budget Statement to come into effect immediately, so long as a single motion moved after the Chancellor's speech is passed. This motion must, however, be approved through the passing of the individual resolutions applying to these taxes within ten days.

The reason for the introduction of the Provisional Collection of Taxes Act 1913 is interesting. One of the most important parliamentary conflicts this century was that fought over the 1909 'People's Budget' of Lloyd George. This Budget Statement was made at the then conventional time in March, but the Finance Bill was not passed by the Commons until November, and was then thrown out by the House of Lords. The Bill occupied seventy days in the House of Commons but never received Royal Assent, so the collection of some taxes that year was perhaps not strictly legitimate. In 1912 this principle was tested by a Conservative back-bencher, Gibson Bowles, when he refused to pay various taxes. He argued that, even though the Commons had passed the Ways and Means resolutions relating to taxation, the Finance Bill had not yet received Royal Assent and so the collection of taxes was illegal. The court agreed with him, and this led to the passing of the Provisional Collection of Taxes Act 1913, which allows the collection, until 5 May, of those taxes that have been continued or amended in the Budget Statement.

THE SUMMER ECONOMIC DEBATE

During the 1980s, the Budget took place in April or May and, at the beginning of each parliamentary session, the Chancellor of the Exchequer gave an Autumn Statement, describing the nation's economic prospects and detailing public expenditure proposals. The Autumn Statement has now been absorbed into the November Budget Statement and is no longer debated separately. The new one-day summer economic debate, which takes place shortly before the House rises in July, is now one of the major debates on the Government's overall strategy. On 12 July 1995, the Chancellor Kenneth Clarke introduced the debate by moving the following motion: That this House welcomes the publication of the Government's latest forecast, which shows growth continuing at a steady and sustainable rate, inflation remaining low, exports rising and Government borrowing falling; and recognizes that this favourable outlook for the economy is a result of the Government's firm commitment to the healthy and sustainable recovery of a modern and competitive industrial economy.

2

THE PALACE AND THE CHAMBER

The two Houses of Parliament are only a part of the Palace of Westminster, which has been a royal palace in one shape or another for 1,000 years. The oldest surviving building within the palace is Westminster Hall, the walls of which were constructed between 1097 and 1099, in the reign of William II. The building of the roof, which is the longest and oldest timber roof in Europe, was supervised by Charles II. The hall has housed the courts of law and many famous trials have been held there, including those of Sir Thomas More, Guy Fawkes, King Charles I and Warren Hastings. Westminster Hall is today used for important ceremonies, such as the Queen's address in 1988 on the tercentenary of the Glorious Revolution, and for lyings in state (the last was in 1965, for Sir Winston Churchill). The palace has not actually been a royal residence since Henry VIII left it, following a fire in 1512, although there is still a bed for the monarch in the Speaker's apartment.

Recently, tennis balls have been found in the rafters that date back to the reign of Henry VIII. They may be testimony of his poor shot in tennis, from those times when he used the hall as his tennis court. Other uses of the hall have not been so well publicized. Upon Charles II's triumphant return to Westminster, one of his first acts was to exhume Oliver Cromwell's body and behead it, before impaling the head on a post which now hangs above the archway leading to the Members' car park. There it remained until, a full year later, a gale blew it from its perch.

The most recent ceremonial use of Westminster Hall was the presentation of addresses to the Queen from both Houses on the fiftieth anniversary of the end of the Second World War (5 May 1995).

During the Second World War, while a fire from an air-raid attack threatened to destroy much of the Palace of Westminster, it was decided to protect the historic hall rather than the more modern debating chamber. As a result, the hall was spared, but the chamber was ruined, and Members of the House of Commons were forced to convene in the corridor and in the House of Lords. As a result, many of Churchill's famous wartime speeches were actually delivered from the House of Lords. But this was not the first time the palace had been destroyed by fire.

Much of the old palace was destroyed in 1834 by a huge fire caused by a stove used to burn Treasury 'tally' sticks (used for accounting). It would not be the last time the Treasury wreaked awesome power over the building and its people.

After the fire a public competition was held to redesign the palace. This was won by Charles Barry and rebuilding (in which he was assisted by A. W. Pugin) began in 1840, and was finished in 1870. The design and architecture of the palace is predominantly Gothic. One effect of the architecture is to convey a completely false sense of antiquity to much of the building. The Members' Lobby and the chamber had to be rebuilt in 1885 after being damaged by a bomb placed there by Irish extremists.

Although the chambers are the most famous parts of the Palace, there are in fact over 1,000 other rooms. There are offices, dining rooms, bars, libraries, committee rooms, private residences for the Speaker and Lord Chancellor, the Members' Lobby and Peers' Lobby, the Central Lobby and many others. Many of these are less than glamorous; at least one MP has called it a Gothic slum. Another Member, Ken Livingstone, found himself without an office for a long time, and many Members find that they must share a small office with another Member.

THE COMMONS CHAMBER

The actual debating chamber is very small indeed. There is room only for 346 of the 651 Members to sit in the benches on the floor of the chamber and room for another ninety-one in the side galleries. If more than this want to be in the chamber, they have to stand behind the Speakers' chair and in the gangways. When full, the drama of the House is enhanced and there is, as Winston Churchill said, 'a sense of crowd and urgency' which intensifies the importance of the event. The chamber of the Commons is very plain compared with the ornateness of that of the Lords. The Speaker sits at one end of the chamber, with the clerks' table in front of his or her chair. The benches on which Members sit run along the length of the chamber, on both sides of the Speaker's chair. The Members of the Government sit to the right-hand side of the Speaker and those of the Opposition to the left. The front bench on the Government's side is called the Treasury Bench, the Prime Minister being the First Lord of the Treasury. Behind this are the Government back benches. The bench immediately behind the Treasury bench is used by ministers' parliamentary private secretaries, who are thus able to deliver messages and advice to their ministers. It was suggested that with the televising of Commons debates, parliament-ary private secretaries would be chosen for their telegenic qualities rather than for anything else. Ironically, the standard television shot of the dispatch box chops the PPSs off at the neck. Similarly, on the other side, there is the Opposition front bench and the back benches.

The reason why the benches in the chamber are arranged opposite each other, in the adversarial style, rather than in the semicircle typical of most legislatures today, lies in the history of the Palace of West-minster. In the sixteenth century, the Commons met in St Stephen's Chapel. The seating in the chapel was arranged in two sets of choir stalls on either side of the altar. When the Commons moved from the chapel they kept to this arrangement, and the tradition survived even the building and rebuilding of the new chamber. This style makes the debate more heated and difficult, as one must constantly be facing one's opponents. But, on the other hand, as many debaters have suggested, this may not be such a bad place for them to be. The only drawback, however, is that you cannot keep an eye on your friends.

At the end of the chamber, opposite the Speaker's chair, is a white line on the carpet known as the Bar. Only Members and certain officers of the House can cross over the Bar into the rest of the chamber, and when they do so by convention they bow to the Speaker's chair.

In front of the Speaker's chair, and separating the two sets of benches, is the table at which three clerks sit. These clerks advise the Speaker and Members on parliamentary procedure. On the table are books, stationery and timing devices, and furthest from the Speaker's chair are two dispatch boxes, one on either side of the table. Front-benchers – either Government Ministers or the principal Opposition spokesmen and women – are able to lean upon their dispatch box when speaking. (When back-benchers speak, they simply stand beside their place on the bench.) The mace also rests on the clerks' table.

Hansard is the official publisher of House of Commons debates, and is named after Mr T. C. Hansard, who first publicized the debates in 1811, and whose family continued to do so for eighty years.

A red line runs along the carpet just in front of both the Treasury bench and the Opposition front bench. These lines are two sword-lengths apart and date from the time when many Members would have carried weapons. Although they were not allowed to bring their swords into the chamber, the red line ensured that, even if some Members broke this rule, fights between Members of opposite sides could still not take place, provided that they kept behind the red lines.

To this day Members should not step forward beyond the red line when they are speaking. The phrase 'toe the line' dates back to the time when risks of a sword fight were higher than they are today. When swords were banned from the chamber, it did not mark the end of violent disputes. There is an engraving of the first fight that broke out in the Commons, over the Irish Home Rule Bill 1889. It shows over twenty Members grabbing each other's clothing and punching each other in the face. Neither did it stop there. In 1972 Ulster MP Bernadette Devlin slapped the Home Secretary's face and pulled his hair. The line still has its uses.

A small gallery to the right of and behind the Speaker's chair, separated from the chamber by a partition, is known as the civil servants' box. Civil servants whose ministers are involved in a debate can sit in the box and pass notes to their minister.

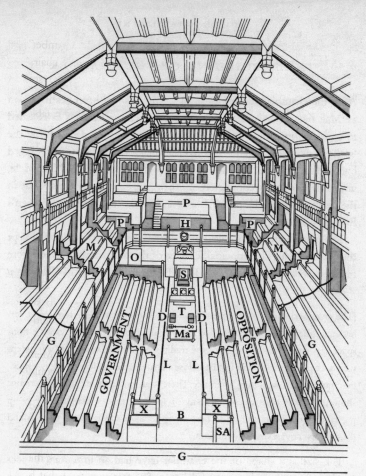

The Chamber of the House of Commons

S Madam Speaker	C Clerks of the House*	X Cross Benches
P Press galleries	T Table of the House	SA Serjeant at Arms
H Hansard Reporters	D Dispatch boxes	M Members' galleries
O Government officials'	Ma Mace†	G Visitors' galleries
Box (advisers to	L Lines‡	
ministers)	B Bar of the House	

* When the House goes into committee, the Speaker leaves the Chair, and the Chairman sits in the chair of the Clerk of the House, which is the one on the left.   † When the House goes into committee, the mace is put 'below the table' on brackets.   ‡ Lines over which Members may not step when speaking from the front benches

THE REBUILDING OF THE CHAMBER

After the chamber of the House of Commons had been destroyed on 10 May 1941 in a German air raid, a select committee was established to consider how the chamber should be rebuilt and it decided that the 'sense of intimacy and almost conversational form of debate encouraged by the dimensions of the old House should be maintained'. Meanwhile, until this work was completed, in 1950, the Commons usually sat in the chamber of the House of Lords and the Lords met in the Queen's Robing Room.

The new chamber was designed by Sir Giles Gilbert Scott, who kept the Gothic style. The principal features of the old chamber, which were retained, were described by Dr Eric Taylor in *The House of Commons at Work*:

[The chamber] had a cosy appearance which was enhanced by the deep over-hanging galleries all round the room and by the fact that all the available floor space was packed with seating of the traditional pew-like variety. It was essentially a chamber which lent itself to close debate, repartee, intervention, rejoinder, rather than sounding rhetoric. There was no rostrum; and experience showed that the consequent necessity of speaking from a bench half-way up the House (the benches rose in tiers on either side) made rolling periods and rousing invective extremely difficult.

The size and shape of the chamber have had an important impact on the nature of parliamentary debates. The fact that the benches are arranged opposite each other, rather than in a semicircle, seems to emphasize the confrontational nature of a two-party political system, which Britain has historically had. However, it is far from certain who the combatants are in parliamentary confrontations. Often friendships exist across the chamber, while rivalries are often most acute between Members of the same party (who are, after all, competitors for advancement). The story is told of a new Tory MP who sat down in the chamber for the first time and remarked, 'It's good to get a sight of the enemy.' For this he was corrected by an older and wiser Conservative Member beside him: 'No, my boy, you've got it wrong. That is the Opposition. Your enemies are behind you.'

The size of the chamber has certainly influenced the atmosphere during important debates. On these occasions the chamber is full, often with many Members standing because there is no room on the benches, and this helps to emphasize the importance of these occasions. When the House is relatively quiet, with perhaps only twenty or thirty Members in the chamber, it does not seem as empty as it would were there 651 seats in the chamber.

GALLERIES

Above the floor of the chamber, there are various galleries. The Strangers' Gallery is above three sides of the chamber, and it is from here that members of the public can watch the proceedings of the House, but they are not allowed to take notes. On the side of the chamber above the Speaker's chair is the Press Gallery, from which journalists can take notes on the debates and reporters from Hansard take substantially verbatim records. A truly verbatim record (like the Hansard of the Saskatchewan Legislature) would be almost unreadable. Hansard reports form the official record of proceedings in the House and they are published after each day as *House of Commons Official Report*. There are similar *Official Reports* for the House of Lords as well as committee proceedings.

Behaviour in the galleries is tightly controlled by the badge messengers, the corps of ex-military warrant officers who run the galleries under the guidance of the Serjeant at Arms. On one occasion, an MP had taken a few guests into the Strangers' Gallery and remained there with them. The debate got exciting, and he started to roar with laughter and generally create great quantities of noise. Within seconds the badge messenger was at his side. 'I don't care how you behave in the chamber, sir,' he said, 'but when you are in the gallery you must behave like an Honourable Gentleman.'

Neither is it just the badge messengers who rule with a rod of iron.

Lord Gowrie, a government minister at the time, was once sitting in the Peers' Gallery with his feet up on the wooden rail – a posture not uncommon in the chamber. The Speaker called a Whip. 'Who is that man?' he demanded. When told, he said, 'Go and tell him to take his feet off my furniture.' The noble Lord did as he was asked.

Amplifiers have been incorporated into the woodwork on the back of each bench. Hence when you see MPs reclining with their feet up, they are not normally sleeping; they are earnestly trying to hear the debate.

COLOUR SCHEME

The benches in the House of Commons are upholstered in green leather – the colour predominant throughout the Commons for carpets, furnishing, notepaper and so on. Red is similarly used in the House of Lords. It is unknown why the Commons chose green in this way, but even in 1663 the benches were upholstered in this colour. It is possible that green was adopted in order to please the Tudor kings, whose livery colours were green and white. Certainly the portcullis, which was an emblem of the Tudors, has become an emblem of the Commons. It is likely that red was selected in the House of Lords because numerous kings have favoured this colour, and it is definitely appropriate to their dignified constitutional function that the Lords have sumptuous reds and golds, while the Commons are surrounded by a more workmanlike green.

3

A DAY IN THE CHAMBER

'If you like life and the human circus, it is hard not to like the House of Commons.' *Woodrow Wyatt*

'I am a Member of Parliament and I work at the House of Commons. You probably all have your own ideas of what the House of Commons is like. It has been described to me as the only lunatic asylum in the country which is run by the inmates.' *Sir Dudley Smith*

Imagine that an MP wants to take up an important issue. Perhaps he wants to correct an apparent injustice, help a constituent or expose what he feels is a Government wrongdoing. He has a variety of options open to him. The most dramatic of these options all focus on the chamber of the House of Commons.

The first step that the MP has to take is to attract attention to the problem – the attention of the public and/or the Government. To achieve this, a skilled MP will often start by looking at the day's order paper. There he may find an opportunity to raise his issue. At the easiest level, he may put a supplementary oral question to a minister. Or he may try to get called to ask one of the Prime Minister. He may decide to attempt something more dramatic – a Private Notice Question or a call for an emergency debate. If it is not urgent but he wants prime-time coverage, he may go for a Ten Minute Rule Bill.

The Government, on the other hand, has a different task. It has more to do but also has more control over the day's proceedings. It may want to communicate good news, or a policy change, or a whole new policy. The Government may 'plant' arranged questions for ministers to answer, make a statement or initiate a full-blooded debate.

The Opposition, meanwhile, wants at every stage to challenge the Government's activities: to argue against its policies, to amend and/or delay its legislation, to cross-examine its ministers. It has its rights also – to a certain amount of time in the chamber, for example. The Opposition can also negotiate various aspects of the way business is handled. (Since the running of the House depends on some degree of co-operation between the two sides, the Opposition always has the threat of withdrawing its co-operation behind any of its demands.)

All of these groups – Government, Opposition and individual back-benchers – look to the order paper to decide their tactics. Many factors – timing, precedence, relevance – will dictate how they achieve their aims.

THE SPEAKER'S PROCESSION

On Monday, Tuesday and Thursday the parliamentary day begins a few minutes before 2.30 p.m., when the Speaker's procession makes its way through the Central Lobby and into the chamber. On Friday, and now Wednesday too, due to recent changes enacted as a result of the Jopling Report recommendations, the House sits from 10 a.m. As the Speaker enters the Central Lobby, one of the policemen on duty there will shout, 'Hats off, strangers.' People wearing hats must remove them, as a sign of respect to the Speaker, and the policemen take off their helmets.

PRAYERS

The Speaker will be in the chamber by 2.30 p.m., at which time her Chaplain reads the prayers. The Speaker and Chaplain kneel at the clerks' table, while the MPs present stand with their backs to the table, a tradition that is said to have originated in the difficulty of kneeling while wearing a sword!

Order of Business
(in the House of Commons)

1 Prayers
2 Queen's answer to addresses
3 Formal communications from the Speaker
4 Motions for unopposed new writs (for by-elections)
5 Private business
6 Motions for unopposed returns
7 Questions for oral answer
8 Private Notice Questions
9 Ministerial statements
10 Introduction of new Members
11 Applications for emergency debates
12 Ceremonial speeches
13 Ballot for Private Member's Motions
14 Personal explanations
15 Considerations of Lords' amendments
16 Matters of parliamentary privilege and opposed by-election writs
17 First reading of public bills
18 Government motions on business of the House
19 Ten Minute Rule Bill
20 Notice of motions on privilege
21 Main business (normally public business)
22 Motion to continue with main business
23 Business not affected by 'moment of interruption'
24 Presentation of public petitions
25 Adjournment motion

PRIVATE BUSINESS

After prayers have been said, members of the public are allowed into the galleries. At this point the Speaker makes whatever formal announcement there may be, such as the death of a Member. A motion may be made at this time to move a writ for a by-election. This motion can be moved at this point only if it is unopposed. (Opposed writs are moved in the time-slot reserved for matters of privilege, immediately before main business.)

Next comes what is known as private business. A private bill promoted by a local authority or a company can be taken through the next stage of the legislative process unless a Member objects, in which case the bill has to be deferred to a later date. On Thursday 13 July 1995, for example, three private bills were read.

QUESTIONS FOR ORAL ANSWER

Questions for oral answer must begin by 2.45 p.m. at the latest, but usually private business takes only a couple of minutes and so questions tend to begin around 2.35 p.m. On 13 July 1995 it was the turn of Treasury Ministers to answer questions on the areas of their responsibility, and this they did until 3.15 p.m.

Question Time can be an occasion for a group of Members to draw the public's attention to an issue that concerns them by repeatedly quizzing the minister on the subject. Alternatively it can be used as a mechanism to demonstrate to the front bench (including the Prime Minister) the strength of back-bench feeling on a subject. For example, on 1989 Budget Day, when the chamber was full and the proceedings were broadcast live, an employment minister had to answer nine questions from Members who wanted the National Dock Labour Scheme to be abolished. The exercise – organized by the author – involved putting between twenty and thirty questions at the Table Office to maximize the chance of the subject being called.

Departmental questions continue on Monday and Wednesday until 3.30 p.m., but at 3.15 p.m. on Tuesday and Thursday it is the turn of the Prime Minister. Again, on 13 July 1995, John Major answered questions for fifteen minutes on a whole range of subjects including British troops in Bosnia, inheritance tax, the rail strike, class sizes, prisoners in Northern Ireland, and trade unions.

PRIVATE NOTICE QUESTIONS

At 3.30 p.m. there may be a Private Notice Question (PNQ), which will be on a subject of urgency. The Speaker decides about noon on the day whether a PNQ will be allowed. On 3 May 1995, for example, there was such a question, when Robin Cook asked the Foreign Secretary to make a statement on the breakdown of the cease-fire in Bosnia. This lasted until 4.08 p.m.

BUSINESS QUESTIONS

There is a particular type of PNQ that is asked each Thursday of the Leader of the House, so that he or she can inform MPs what business the House will be dealing with in the following week. As the day being described – 13 July 1995 – was a Thursday, the Leader of the House, Tony Newton, described the following week's business in response to a question asked by the shadow leader, Ann Taylor. This procedure allows Members to raise matters that interest them, on the pretext of asking the Leader of the House to allow debates on that subject. On 13 July 1995, this lasted for about half an hour.

MINISTERIAL STATEMENTS

After Private Notice Questions, there may be a ministerial statement (these usually precede Business Questions). The Government may wish to announce some new policy or to state its views and proposed actions on some occurrence – a major accident or terrorist incident, for example. On 13 July 1995, the Secretary of State for Defence, Michael Portillo, made an announcement about Government orders for defence equipment. It is the Government's right to make such statements and it does not need the permission of the House or the Speaker. Normally it will inform the Speaker, and the statement will be announced on the Commons annunciator system at 1 p.m.

OTHER MATTERS

Various other matters can be dealt with between the end of Question Time and the main business of the day. For example, a new MP elected at a by-election would be introduced at this point. He or she either swears an oath of loyalty to the monarch or makes an affirmation of loyalty, then signs the roll and shakes the Speaker's hand.

APPLICATIONS FOR EMERGENCY DEBATES

Also at this time of day Members may make a three-minute speech arguing that an emergency debate should be granted by the Speaker under Standing Order No. 20 (SO No. 20). Very few of these requests are ever granted. Nevertheless, the three minutes of prime parliamentary time can be very effective in highlighting a problem.

One occasion when the Speaker, Bernard Weatherill, *did* grant an SO No. 20 was during the furore in 1988 over the social security reforms. Although he was criticized on the Government side for it, he probably judged that granting such a motion would help vent the anger of the Opposition in a more constructive way than the parliamentary guerrilla activity that would otherwise have followed.

Meanwhile, in the division lobbies, there may also be a ballot in order to decide which back-benchers are allowed to decide the topics for debate on days set aside for back-benchers' debates. The draw is made and the result announced in the chamber.

Private Members' motions (and ballots) have been discontinued for the duration of the Jopling experiment.

FIRST READING OF PUBLIC BILLS

The next business is to give a first reading to public bills, but this is only a formality and takes little time. Other business that might follow after this includes the allocation of work to standing committees, Government motions to suspend the standing orders, so that the agenda for business for the House that day may be changed, and the proposal of a Ten Minute Rule Bill (each Tuesday and Wednesday, usually from the seventh week of the session).

PARLIAMENTARY PRIVILEGE

Before moving on to the main business of the day, it is also possible that a matter of parliamentary privilege be debated, although such debates are exceedingly rare.

MAIN BUSINESS

The House now proceeds to the main business of the day, which, on 13 July 1995, consisted of two debates on Select Committee reports relating to social security and animal diseases respectively. Usually main business carries on until 10 p.m. There are, however, a number of days on which main business is interrupted at 7 p.m. by what is known as opposed private business, so that MPs can debate private legislation.

On 13 July 1995, main business continued until 10 p.m. Motions were then moved by Government Whips that Statutory Instruments relating to contracting out, European budgets and public health be approved.

At 10 p.m. main business ends with the 'moment of interruption', when the Speaker stands and calls, 'Order, order'. The vote needs to be taken before the moment of interruption, otherwise the business is talked out (the closure can be claimed at the 'moment of interruption', but this is too technical a point with which to burden the reader). Generally the vote on that business is then held. The parliamentary day is still not over, however. If the Government puts a motion to suspend the Ten o'clock Rule, main business can be continued. There are also certain proceedings that are unaffected by the 'moment of interruption', such as consideration of the Finance Bill, of European Community documents (which are given one and a half hours' debate after 10 p.m.) and of Statutory Instruments. Before the Jopling changes, the House would typically rise between midnight and 1 a.m. from Monday to Thursday. Since the start of the Jopling experiment in January 1995, some of the time pressures have been removed: Wednesday sittings have largely removed the need for late sittings on Thursday. The Government proposed to use its best endeavours to avoid late sittings whenever possible.

As a result, the Ten o'clock Rule has been suspended less frequently, and less exempted business has been taken after 10 p.m. EC documents and affirmative Statutory Instruments are automatically referred to standing committees (by a standing order and a sessional order respectively), unless deferred by the Government. The average time of the House rising is now shortly before 11 p.m.

PETITIONS

When the main business of the day has finished, petitions can be presented formally. Historically, petitions have offered people the opportunity to inform Parliament about personal grievances. However, Parliament did not always pay much attention to petitions; the official *Journal* of 10 December 1640 records that a committee was set up to consider a particular petition:

that was inclosed in the cover of a letter, addressed to the Parliament, and found upon Salisbury Plain; and being brought to the Mayor of Salisbury, was by him sent up to Serjeant Hide, a member of this House, and by him this Day offered to the House. The Committee, after they had pursued it, found it of no better consequence than to be burnt.

ADJOURNMENT MOTIONS

There were no petitions on 13 July 1995, and so the House finally moved to the daily adjournment debate, which – unless it begins before 10 p.m. – lasts for up to half an hour. This procedure allows Members to bring up a matter of local or personal interest. On 13 July 1995, for example, the Conservative Member Anthony Coombs drew to the attention of a Home Office Minister the condition of the probation service in Hereford and Worcester. The daily adjournment debate normally consists only of a speech by the back-bencher proposing the motion and a reply from the relevant Minister. On 13 July, the debate finished at 10.30 p.m. and the House adjourned. When the House rises, police around the palace shout, 'Who goes home?' This is a tradition that began in the days when Members would leave in groups so as not to have to walk on their own over the poorly lit and dangerous fields that then joined Westminster and the City.

ALL-NIGHT SITTINGS

Since the Jopling changes, Parliament has often risen by 10.30 p.m., and all-night sittings are rare. But this was not always the case. Between 1979 and 1988, for example, there were seven occasions on which a single sitting lasted more than twenty-four hours. If one day's business continues until past the time at which the next day's business is due to start, that day's business is then lost. The record for the longest sitting was on the Protection of Person and Property (Ireland) Bill 1881: this lasted for forty-one and a half hours.

THE JOPLING COMMITTEE

To solve the problem of late-night sittings, and because of an increased work schedule and other clerical burdens, a committee was established in July 1991, chaired by Michael Jopling MP, to evaluate the procedures of the House of Commons. In January 1995, many of its suggestions were implemented: these included the introduction of Wednesday morning sittings, ten non-sitting Fridays in each session to allow Members to return to their constituencies (which they had already tended to do when there was no Thursday night division), stricter time limits and a better budgeting of the House's time.

On Wednesdays, the House now meets at 10 a.m. (rather than 2.30 p.m.). Debates on general topics, with a time limit of one and a half hours, continue until 1 p.m. following the procedures used in the post-Consolidated Fund debates (see page 73). Between 1 p.m. and 2 p.m. the procedure for the daily half-hour adjournment debate is followed and at 2.30 p.m., after a half-hour break, the House proceeds to the business normally taken after prayers, going straight on to questions. Unlike Fridays, there is no provision for the Speaker to interrupt proceedings at 11 a.m. for Private Notice Questions or statements – these will all take place at 3.30 p.m.

Also under the new changes, provisions for Private Members' motions on ten Fridays and two Monday afternoons have been discontinued, and adjournment debates no longer follow the Consolidated Fund Bill debate. All these changes – some of which may seem relatively minor – were designed to remove the need for late-night sittings and many of the Friday debates.

FRIDAY

The timetable of the House of Commons on Friday is different from that of other weekdays, because Friday is the day when most Members leave Westminster to spend the weekend in their constituencies. On

Friday the House meets between 9.30 a.m. and 2.30 p.m. There are no questions (apart from Private Notice Questions), no private business and no requests for emergency debates. Petitions are taken at the start rather than the end of the day and on occasions the presentation of multiple petitions has delayed main business significantly. (Indeed, this is now a standard tactic to help 'talk out' a controversial Private Member's Bill.) The presentation of petitions on a Friday can also give them rather more publicity, since they are early in the day.

If there is a Private Notice Question or a ministerial statement, it is heard at 11 a.m. Friday is the day for Private Members' Bills or motions. Many Private Members' Bills deal with matters of social or moral importance, rather than party politics, and so they may be extremely controversial. This can lead to the use of some fierce and apparently undemocratic tactics. On Government-controlled Fridays, only uncontroversial measures are usually discussed. Since the Jopling changes, the presentation of petitions can now continue beyond 10 a.m. on Private Members' Fridays.

WRITS

While writs for by-elections are usually moved by the Chief Whip of the departed Member's party, this is not always the case and they can be used for purposes of delay, as was attempted by Jim Sillars on Budget Day 1989 (see page 52). This tactic is especially effective on Friday. If a writ is moved on Private Members' day and is opposed, proceedings lapse.

Dennis Skinner has twice moved motions for writs to be issued. Both occasions were on Friday mornings because Dennis Skinner wanted to obstruct the progress of two Private Members' Bills. The motion that a writ should be issued can be made without any prior notice, and on a Friday such a motion has precedence over almost all other business. On 7 June 1985 Dennis Skinner moved the writ for the Brecon and Radnor by-election, and was thus able to prevent the passage of a Private Member's Bill on research on human embryos.

He also moved the writ for the Richmond, Yorkshire, by-election in January 1989 as a tactic to defeat Ann Widdecombe's controversial bill on abortion. As part of his delaying tactics, Dennis Skinner discussed numerous factors that related (directly, indirectly and often very indirectly) to the writ for the Richmond by-election. While Dennis Skinner's tactics were successful, they were by no means popular with all MPs. Sir Peter Emery commented:

It is unique for such a debate to take place on the moving of a writ. This is being used as a dilatory motion to frustrate a Private Member's time. All Private Members normally wish to safeguard that time. Although the Hon. Gentleman has been very humorous, this act of procedure does not help the House generally. It does not help the House's reputation and will not be understood by people outside this House.

This question of whether or not such time-wasting tactics to block bills is democratic is frequently discussed in Westminster. What it means is that controversial legislation with a determined minority opposing it cannot expect to pass through the House, unless the Government makes time for it. Although the Government did make time for David Steel's bill legalizing abortion, it was an unusual measure. In effect this problem caused by time-wasting reduces the role of Private Members' Bills to that of implementing only matters of broad public consensus with little opposition.

MPS' WORKLOAD

It is important to remember that the business carried out on the floor of the House is only one part of an MP's workload. Before the House rises, he or she may have read and answered their mail, spent some time researching or writing a speech, met with constituents or representatives of a pressure group, and had a working lunch (or even the awful modern innovation of a working breakfast). There are also media interviews, meetings with back-benchers and committee work to be fitted into their daily schedule. A fourteen-hour day is the norm from

Monday to Thursday, in addition to whatever the Member does in his or her constituency.

A DAY IN THE LORDS

The Lords meet in a similar way to the Commons, albeit for fewer days in the year. They also meet in the mornings for judicial business – hearing appeals, typically. This, the very pinnacle of our legal process, is carried out by the Appellate Committees, which consist solely of specially appointed, salaried legal Lords called Lords of Appeal in Ordinary.

The public business of the House of Lords starts at 2.30 p.m. and follows an order of business similar to that of the Commons.

Order of Business
(in the House of Lords)

1 Prayers
2 Introduction
3 Oaths of allegiance
4 Messages from the Crown
5 Royal Assent
6 Addresses of congratulation or sympathy to the Crown
7 Obituary tributes
8 Personal statements
9 Starred questions
10 Private Notice Questions
11 Questions of privilege
12 Statements on business (of the House)
13 Ministerial statements
14 Presentation and first reading of public bills
15 Messages from the Commons
16 Private bills
17 Presentation of public petitions

18 Business of the House motions
19 Motions relating to chairman of committees' business
20 Motions for the appointment of select committees
21 Public bills, measures and affirmative instruments
22 Other motions
23 Unstarred questions

Like it, too, most of the items occur only rarely, while a few, such as questions and public business, occur every day. The principal difference is the Peers' attitude to parliamentary time. Questions are limited by number (normally four) not time, and in theory any number of supplementaries can be asked. There is no 'moment of interruption', and debates go on until they stop, irrespective of time.

4

PARLIAMENTARY QUESTIONS

QUESTION TIME

Question Time constitutes only one-tenth of parliamentary business but it is undoubtedly the most exciting tenth, so it occupies a disproportionate amount of parliamentary time on radio and television. Theoretically it is the time in which both Government and Opposition back-benchers are able to bring the actions of Government ministers under scrutiny and challenge. As well as entailing a large amount of back-bench involvement, Question Time also enables all Members to score political points and is therefore seen very much as a political battlefield. To comprehend how this battle is fought, we have to understand the rules that it is fought by. It helps, too, to understand its history.

The practice of questioning ministers evolved only gradually. Not until 1833 were ministers given advance notice of the questions they were to be asked, when the questions were printed on the notice paper of forthcoming business; and it was only in 1869 that the questions were all grouped together in a special section of the notice paper.

Question Time has since developed into an important part of parliamentary life. Each year about 40,000 questions are asked by MPs to ministers; of this figure around 5,000 are answered orally, while the rest receive written replies. To assist back-bench and Opposition scrutiny of the executive, all these answers, both oral and written, are printed in Hansard, the daily record on what has been said in the House. In the 1993–4 session there were 41,508 written questions, 5,535 oral questions and 851 Private Notice Questions.

TYPES OF QUESTION

There are three types of question asked in conventional Question Time in the House of Commons: oral questions (which are answered actually in the chamber), written questions (which receive written answers) and questions for written answer on a named day (which the department concerned must have at least two days to answer). Via an arranged question, it is also possible to have a short statement made to the House of Commons which is also to be made elsewhere – in the Lords, for example. This is often done as a courtesy to the Commons.

Oral Question Time usually occupies around fifty-five minutes, from about 2.35 to 3.30 p.m. every Monday to Thursday of each sitting week. There is a rota by which each Government department has to answer questions every three or four weeks. The table (see pages 49–51) shows a typical two-month rota with the priority department for questions marked in bold. MPs submit oral questions in writing to the clerks a fortnight before they are due to be answered. The questions are shuffled together and picked out to determine in what order they will be asked. Prime Minister's Question Time is even shorter, comprising a fifteen-minute period twice a week on Tuesday and Thursday afternoons.

PRIVATE NOTICE QUESTIONS

A particular type of question is the Private Notice Question (PNQ), which allows MPs to raise urgent questions to a minister at very short notice indeed. If a member wishes to ask a PNQ he or she must apply to the Speaker before noon and, if the Speaker considers that the matter is sufficiently important and urgent, she will inform the relevant department at once. The MP then asks the question in the House at 3.30 p.m. immediately after conventional questions. Recent PNQs have concerned, for example, the miners' strike, a dock strike, floods in Mozambique, terrorism in Northern Ireland and salmonella in eggs. During the 1982–3 session, only seven PNQs were asked; however,

Order of Questions
Tuesday 6 June – Thursday 27 July 1995

Note: Questions for oral answer should usually be submitted between 10 a.m. and 5 p.m., exactly a fortnight before the date of answer, in order to be included in the random shuffle to determine the order of questions. Where the House is adjourned for more than two days, tabling dates are in accordance with paragraphs (7) and (8) of Standing Order No. 18.

1. Starting not later than 3.10 p.m.   2. Starting not later than 3.15 p.m.   3. Starting not later than 3.20 p.m.   4. Starting not later than 3.25 p.m.   5. Also answers on behalf of Lord Advocate.   6. Includes questions to the Finance and Services Committee.

Tues. 6 June	Wed. 7 June	Thurs. 8 June
Defence	Foreign & Commonwealth (other than Overseas Development Questions)	Agriculture, Fisheries & Food
At 3.15 p. m. **Prime Minister**		At 3.15 p. m. **Prime Minister**

Mon. 12 June	Tues. 13 June	Wed. 14 June	Thurs. 15 June
Wales Chancellor of the Duchy of Lancaster[1]	Employment	Trade & Industry	Treasury
At 3.15 p. m. **Prime Minister**			At 3.15 p. m. **Prime Minister**

Mon. 19 June	Tues. 20 June	Wed. 21 June	Thurs. 22 June
Social Security	Health	Environment	Home Office
Public Accounts Commission[1]			
House of Commons Commission[2,6]			
Lord President of the Council[4]	At 3.15 p.m. Prime Minister		At 3.15 p.m. Prime Minister

Mon. 26 June	Tues. 27 June	Wed. 28 June	Thurs. 29 June
National Heritage	Education	Scotland[5]	Northern Ireland
Attorney General[1]			
Foreign & Commonwealth (Overseas Development Questions)[3]	At 3.15 p.m. Prime Minister		At 3.15 p.m. Prime Minister

Mon. 3 July	Tues. 4 July	Wed. 5 July	Thurs. 6 July
Transport	Defence	Foreign & Commonwealth (other than Overseas Development)	Agriculture, Fisheries & Food
Chancellor of the Duchy of Lancaster[1]			
	At 3.15 p.m. Prime Minister		At 3.15 p.m. Prime Minister

Mon. 10 July	Tues. 11 July	Wed. 12 July	Thurs. 13 July
Wales	Employment	Trade & Industry	Treasury
Church Commissioners[1]			
Lord Chancellor's Department[2]			
	At 3.15 p.m. Prime Minister		At 3.15 p.m. Prime Minister

Mon. 17 July	Tues. 18 July	Wed. 19 July	Thurs. 20 July
Social Security	Health	Environment	Home Office
Attorney General[1]			
Foreign & Commonwealth (Overseas Development Questions)[3]			
	At 3.15 p.m. Prime Minister		At 3.15 p.m. Prime Minister

Mon. 24 July	Tues. 25 July	Wed. 26 July	Thurs. 27 July
National Heritage	Education	Scotland[5]	Northern Ireland
Chancellor of the Duchy of Lancaster[1]			
	At 3.15 p.m. Prime Minister		At 3.15 p.m. Prime Minister

in recent parliamentary sessions, there has been an average of about four to five each month.

The initiator of a PNQ is often the front-bench spokesman or woman of one of the Opposition parties. More and more these days, the PNQ is used as a tactic to force a short debate, in media prime time. The subjects are highly topical issues that are generally potentially embarrassing to the Government.

An unusual use of a PNQ occurred on 1989 Budget Day. It was known in advance that a Scottish Nationalist, Jim Sillars, was going to try to pre-empt the Chancellor's Statement, by moving a writ for the Glasgow Central by-election and, while so doing, talk about matters of interest to the Celtic Nationalist parties. Had he been successful, he would have had an enormous audience of people who had tuned in via television and radio in order to hear the Budget.

Both front benches were opposed to this tactic, and they found a way of trumping it. The then Leader of the Opposition, Neil Kinnock, asked the Chancellor a PNQ. This was because opposed by-election writs are dealt with after questions, and so the Chancellor would be able to make his Budget Statement as the answer to Neil Kinnock's PNQ, thus preventing Jim Sillars from raising his writ, or even a point of order. When Jim Sillars refused to accept the Speaker's ruling that he would have to wait until after the PNQ before moving that the writ be issued, the Speaker had to 'name' Jim Sillars. The House then voted to suspend him and moved on to Neil Kinnock's PNQ and, with it, the Budget.

On Thursday every week that Parliament is sitting, the Leader of the House is asked a PNQ by the Shadow Leader of the House about the business that the House will be considering during the following week. This query is raised in the form of a PNQ to ensure that it is dealt with straight after conventional questions. Very occasionally, when a senior Cabinet minister has an urgent statement to make, business questions are downgraded to a statement to allow the urgent statement to go first out of convenience.

PROCEDURE

Although there is a fortnight's notice for oral questions, and the answers can be well prepared, the questioner may, during Question Time itself, ask a supplementary question for which no notice is given. It is therefore common for vague or open questions to be asked first, with the questioner following up with a quite specific supplementary. For example, Mrs Thatcher was once asked if she had any plans to make an official visit to Gidea Park. After her reply that she had no such plans, the supplementary question was asked: 'If the Prime Minister is making a journey to Gidea Park, will she take with her today's edition of the *Evening Standard* and read the article that points out that building society mortgage money will be in very short supply.' Open questions to departmental ministers (as opposed to the Prime Minister) are actively discouraged, and the Speaker would not call any supplementaries.

When Question Time starts, the Speaker calls the Member whose question is first on the Order Paper. The Member stands up and says, 'Number One, Madam Speaker' and the minister then answers the question of that number. As the minister sits down, Members who wish to ask supplementaries to that question stand up to try to catch the Speaker's eye. This is usually when the fun starts. Invariably the Member who asked the original question is called first. The Speaker will usually allow a few supplementary questions and, since ministers cannot prepare for all possible questions, they may have to answer without guidance from their department and may make a mistake. The Opposition Members may try to trip ministers into an embarrassing disclosure or commitment or may attempt to highlight weaknesses in Government policy. Generally, although by no means always, Government back-benchers will try to ask supplementaries that allow ministers to show the stronger aspects of Government policy or highlight weaknesses in Opposition policy.

Do not imagine, however, that the casualties are all on one side. Ministers are very canny operators and can bite back. Gerald Kaufman once described in *How to be a Minister* how he dealt with a slightly difficult opponent:

If you have any sense, search your political memory for weak points in the parliamentary record of any troublesome Opposition Member and prepare to floor him if you can manage it. When the Department of Industry (that is, in this case, myself) was having to consider whether to renew the licence which allowed the Hull City Council, alone in the country, to run its own telephone service independently of the Post Office a Conservative Member of Parliament, Michael Neubert, put down a question about it.

I recollected hazily in my mind that he had once voted against a Private Member's Bill put forward by a Labour MP which aimed at extending the powers of local councils to run commercial services. The Department of the Environment confirmed this from its records, so that when Neubert asked his expected supplementary question championing the renewal of Hull's licence I was able to remind him of his earlier misdeed and welcome his conversion to municipal Socialism. That got no one anywhere, but was at any rate good clean fun and went down well with Hull's Labour MPs.

The other problem that faces a back-bencher is topicality. 'A week is a long time in politics,' as Harold Wilson said, but two weeks elapse between the submission of the question and its answer in the chamber. The result is that Members often try to get a topical supplementary on a matter that was not even known when the original question was asked. Getting in a supplementary on, say, nuclear waste to an original question on, say, dustbins can be akin to making a silk purse from the proverbial sow's ear.

PRIME MINISTER'S QUESTION TIME

The adversarial nature of Parliament is most evident during Prime Minister's Question Time. This is because it is the 'clash of the giants'; because it can address the issues most controversial on any day; because it get most press, radio and TV coverage; and because its rules allow maximum scope for surprise or 'ambush' questions. The questions and answers to be heard in Prime Minister's Question Time are rarely simple matters of information. Nor should they be expected to be.

Even before Prime Minister's Question Time, the 'clash of giants' between the Prime Minister and Leader of the Opposition was more newsworthy than it was informative:

GLADSTONE: Mr Disraeli cannot possibly be sure of the facts.

DISRAELI: I wish that I could be as sure of anything as my opponent is of everything.

The purpose of most of the questions asked to the Prime Minister is to make a political point. An example of this followed the publicity given to the temporary detention of the Leader of the Opposition, Neil Kinnock, by the Zimbabwean army when he visited that country. At the next Prime Minister's Question Time, a Conservative back-bencher asked Mrs Thatcher whether she will 'take time to ask the Zimbabwe Government whether they would commend the Lance Corporal who refused to be bullied –' At this point the MP was stopped by the Speaker, who explained that this was not a matter for which the Prime Minister had responsibility. Mrs Thatcher was nevertheless able to use her answer to make a joke at the expense of Neil Kinnock:

THE PRIME MINISTER (MRS MARGARET THATCHER): Our Consular services and Embassies are well satisfied and able to deal with almost any situation. The aid that we give to the front-line states is greatly appreciated, as is the training that we give in Zimbabwe to the armed forces of that country.

The rules and tactics that govern Prime Minister's Questions are still evolving, as it has only existed in the current format since 1961. When this format was first introduced, Prime Ministers would deflect all questions that related to an individual department to the relevant minister. Thus open questions were developed.

There is undoubtedly a large element of gamesmanship involved in oral Question Time in the Commons. A particularly good example of this came in December 1965, when the Labour Prime Minister, Harold Wilson, was asked by a Conservative MP if a speech made by the Foreign Secretary on the issue of European unity accurately expressed the Government's policy. After answering that it did, Harold Wilson was asked a supplementary question, to which he replied:

THE PRIME MINISTER (MR HAROLD WILSON): Entry into the EEC is not open to us in existing circumstances and no question of fresh negotiations can arise at present. We shall work with our EFTA partners through the Council of Europe and through WEU, for the closest possible relations with the Six consistent with our Commonwealth ties.

Harold Wilson's answer put an end to questions by Conservatives on this topic because it was a direct quotation from the 1964 Conservative election manifesto.

THE INFLUENCE OF THE SPEAKER

Speakers can markedly influence the flavour of Question Time. They select the supplementaries to questions which are called, a process which in practice is entirely random. The 'shuffle' can even be witnessed by MPs, if they so choose. Nevertheless, in an analysis of the results by Robert Hayward, MP, minority party questions seem to come high on the order paper a disproportionate number of times. This is a coincidence, and does not prove that the shuffle is somehow rigged in favour of the minority parties.

Speakers, however, certainly influence the tone – and the pressure on the minister – by the pace at which they take the House through the questions on the order paper. Speaker Selwyn Lloyd, as an experienced ex-minister, knew that ministers received the toughest grilling when the Speaker allowed numerous supplementaries. Members could then force a minister into a corner and into facing embarrassing failures or inconsistencies. He, therefore, in his constitutional role as defender of back-benchers' interests, allowed many supplementaries on each question but, accordingly, called fewer principal questions. Speaker Weatherill – also seen as a trenchant defender of back-bench as against Government interests – was in a similar mould. Speaker Thomas, however, allowed fewer supplementaries but as a result covered more subjects.

Clearly, it is very important to attract the attention of the Speaker. Different people do it in different ways. Obviously, when you are already famous it is not a problem, but 'new boys' may have difficulty getting called both for questions and for speeches. This is particularly true in Question Time, when the Speaker does not have a list of the people she intends to call other than the askers of individual questions. Methods vary; there are those whose natural attributes draw attention to themselves.

In the 1994–95 Parliament, attracting the Speaker's attention was rarely a problem for the Labour MP and former actor Andrew Faulds, with his stentorian roar and immense character, or for the Conservative MP David Evans, giving his own brand of barbed homespun wisdom at full volume. Height and corpulence can also be an advantage in catching the Speaker's eye. Those less well equipped have been known to draw attention to themselves by a variety of other methods, including brilliantly coloured garments, ties and even socks displayed in the prevailing parliamentary procedure of putting one's feet on the benches in front. Dennis Skinner, the so-called 'Beast of Bolsover', will leap to his feet and, with very sharp timing, interject a one-liner before anyone is called. By such methods are reputations made (and destroyed).

As a more general rule, in debates as well as questions, Privy Councillors have precedence over others in seeking to catch the Speaker's eye.

RULES AND TACTICS

There are various rules that govern which questions can be asked by MPs. Questions should, in general, be fairly short and topical and should not be rhetorical or hypothetical. They should be concerned with facts rather than with arguments or opinions. Questions are not allowed to criticize various individuals or institutions, including the Royal Family, heads of state, the decisions of either House of Parliament and the courts. They must relate only to those areas over which the minister has official responsibility.

Much of the point-scoring involves clever tactics on the part of individual back-benchers to portray their concerns within the rules of the House. These rules are most important where they restrict the supplementary question. In most cases the supplementary must relate to the original question and to the minister's responsibilities. Clearly most scope for an 'ambush' question exists in questions to the Prime Minister, who has responsibilities for all actions of the Government. This is particularly true for an open question.

There are, therefore, rules that limit questions put to the Prime Minister, and new MPs have to tread warily if they are not to incur an intervention from the Speaker. A good example of this arose on 7 June 1988, when a new Member, Tim Janman, wanted to use Prime Minister's Question Time to attack the Opposition's policy on defence, which at that time was a matter of some controversy. The exchange in the Chamber went as follows:

MR TIM JANMAN: Will my Right Hon. Friend agree that the Opposition's policies on defence are clearly divided –

MR SPEAKER: Order. The Hon. Gentleman must ask a question for which the Prime Minister has responsibility.

MR JANMAN: In her busy day will my Right Hon. Friend consider that the Opposition's policies on defence –

MR SPEAKER: Order. I cannot allow the Hon. Gentleman to continue along that line.

Tim Janman's mistake was to address a matter that was not the responsibility of the Prime Minister but that of the Opposition. Even so, clever tactics can still win the day. This was demonstrated by the same MP in a courageous second intervention later in the week:

MR TIM JANMAN: Given our long-standing commitment to the independent nuclear deterrent, our recently announced support for the European fighter aircraft programme and our continuing full implementation of the armed forces pay review body recommendations, does my Right Hon. Friend agree that the Government's defence policies are intellectually well founded, firm and consistent, unlike the increasingly divided, indecisive and floundering policies of the Opposition.

THE PRIME MINISTER (MRS MARGARET THATCHER): Yes, our defence policies effectively safeguard the defence of this country and ensure that we are staunch allies of NATO, including its vital nuclear deterrent policy. I have not been able to make out the Opposition's policy. I do not believe that it has changed from having absolute unilateral nuclear disarmament and no nuclear deterrent.

In essence, Tim Janman asked the same question on both occasions, but only on the second occasion did the majority of it relate to Government policy and did he phrase it so that an attack on the Opposition's policy was at the very end of his question – indeed, the word 'Opposition' was the very last word. As a result, by the time the Speaker realized the thrust of the question the Prime Minister was already on her feet giving her answer. This is an excellent example of how simple tactical devices can be used by back-benchers to make their point in the chamber.

Questions cannot be asked on something over which the minister has no control – for example, the accuracy of press reports or statements by private citizens. Those on nationalized industries or the recently privatised agencies must be concerned with general policy rather than with their day-to-day administration. Nor is it permissible to ask questions about matters that are under trial or that are being used to advertise something. In fact, MPs are not allowed to ask questions on about 100 subjects, including the secret services, aspects of defence and confidential commercial information. However, the relevant minister can be asked once each session if he or she is now willing to answer questions on previously disallowed subjects. Furthermore, once a question has been answered fully, it cannot be asked again during the same session. Even if a minister has refused to give some information or take some action, the same question cannot be asked for the next three months.

The minister might not explicitly refuse to answer a question but may deflect it, often with a witticism or an attack on the Opposition, or both. Sir Winston Churchill was not unskilled at this:

MR ARTHUR LEWIS: Is the Prime Minister aware of the deep concern felt by the people of this country at the whole question of the Korean conflict?

THE PRIME MINISTER (SIR WINSTON CHURCHILL): I am fully aware of the deep concern felt by the Hon. Member in many matters above his comprehension.

MPs have no right to insist that a minister answers any particular question. The first recorded ruling on questions, by Speaker Cornwall in 1783, was that a minister had the right to answer, or not to answer, every question as he thought proper. For example, when one MP complained, on 8 July 1943, that a minister had not answered his question, he was told that the minister's reply had run to nine lines in Hansard. Of course, receiving an answer to a question and having the question answered are two entirely different things.

As a political institution the House is not run in quite the same way as a conventional court of law. This was summarized by the early twentieth-century Prime Minister A. J. Balfour:

It has always been desirable to tell the truth, but seldom if ever necessary to tell the whole truth...

In 1894, when Rosebery in his first speech as Prime Minister caused a storm by describing England in relation to Ireland as 'the predominant partner', he asked Campbell-Bannerman, in some perplexity, why this remark had stirred up such a shemozzle. He pointed out that it was, after all, true. Campbell-Bannerman used to enjoy telling this story afterwards. It showed, he said, how little political and parliamentary education Rosebery had had if he thought it a sufficient defence of any public utterance that it was true.

A question may actually not receive any answer beyond the bald statement that the information requested is 'not available', 'not centrally recorded', or that to give an answer would not be 'in the public interest' or 'in accordance with normal practice', or 'confidential' or 'classified' or is available 'only at disproportionate cost'. Occasionally this can be quite ridiculous. Questions that relate to expenditure of many billions of pounds may not be answered because they might cost a few hundred pounds. However, those are Parliament's rules and it would be surprising if ministers did not use them to their advantage from time to time:

Mr Tony Banks asked the Prime Minister what is the sum above which an answer to a parliamentary question is considered to represent disproportional cost.

THE PRIME MINISTER (MRS MARGARET THATCHER): It is for the Minister to decide whether to decline to answer a question on grounds of disproportional cost. Any question likely to cost more than £200 is referred to the responsible minister before significant resources are committed.

Mr Tony Banks asked the Prime Minister how many questions she had refused to answer since 1979 on the grounds of disproportional cost.

THE PRIME MINISTER: This information can only be supplied at disproportionate cost.

The disproportionate cost limit in 1995 is £450.

STRESSES AND STRAINS

The first time a new minister has to answer questions from the dispatch box is a very frightening occasion for the minister. Most ministers have the grace to admit this and many will also agree that it continues to be very stressful. Both the ministers and the House treat the session with proper respect, more than one minister having been seen sprinting down a corridor so as not to be late for parliamentary questions. This is as it should be. Question Time is the occasion at which back-benchers can challenge the power of Government on reasonably equal terms and ministers should therefore be on their mettle.

Ministers are, of course, backed by the resources of their departments. Sometimes, however, even this breaks down.

Question 29   MR MARK FISHER: To ask the Under-Secretary of State for the Arts when he intends to reply to the report from the Education, Science and Arts Committee on the public and private funding of the arts.

THE UNDER-SECRETARY OF STATE FOR THE ARTS (MR WILLIAM WAL-
DEGRAVE): The Hon. Member will have noticed that my brief runs only up
to question 28 –

[*Laughter*]

MR DENNIS CANAVAN: Resign.

On this occasion the House accepted the freely admitted mistake with
honour and good grace.

The number of people who have collapsed at the dispatch box
demonstrates that the stress is truly enormous. For example, the Under-
Secretary of State for Wales, Michael Roberts, died in February 1983 in
the middle of responding to Welsh Labour Members. Technically no
MP officially dies in the Palace of Westminster. Instead the Member
is always deemed to have died *en route* to the hospital. This may seem
a morbid reference here, but physical collapse at the dispatch box is
more common than might be supposed. Although there are clearly
other reasons, the fact that the collapse actually happens at that time
and place is an indication of just how tough it really is.

THE HOUSE OF LORDS

Both oral and written questions feature in the House of Lords though
some of the procedures are different from those in the Commons.

Obviously there is no Prime Minister's Question Time in the House
of Lords, as the convention has, during this century, become that the
Prime Minister must be a Member of the House of Commons. The
total number of questions put to Government ministers by peers is
only a fraction of the number asked in the Commons: in the 1985–6
session, for example, the total number was less than 2,000, of which
almost two-thirds were written questions. All the questions and answers
in the House of Lords are printed in Hansard. The most common
types of oral question are known as starred questions because they are
printed on the order paper with an asterisk alongside them. At the
beginning of each sitting day in the Lords, up to four such questions

can be asked of the Government. Unlike in the Commons, there is no rota of days on which a particular department can be questioned and so a peer can ask a starred question of any Government department on any day. Starred questions may not be used to initiate a debate.

Another form of oral question is the unstarred question, which may start a full debate and is taken when the House has finished its other business for the day.

As in the House of Commons, Private Notice Questions exist in the Lords but they are quite rare. A PNQ was asked in 1986, but the previous one to that had been during the 1983–4 session. The Leader of the House decides whether a proposed PNQ can be asked. However, when the Opposition in the Lords requests it, the answers to many PNQs asked in the Commons are read out as Government statements in the Lords.

5

DEBATES

'Votes are to swords exactly what banknotes are to gold – the
one is effective only because the other is believed to lie behind
it.'   *F. E. Smith, Earl of Birkenhead*

RULES AND CONVENTIONS

To an outsider, maybe the strangest features of the House are the rules
and conventions that must be adhered to by MPs when they are
speaking in a debate. For example, when other MPs are being referred
to, they must be addressed in the third person, according to either the
office they hold or the constituency they represent. So, if an MP was
talking about John Major, he or she might refer to him as 'the Prime
Minister' or as the 'Right Honourable Member for Huntingdon'. Privy
Councillors are referred to as 'Right Honourable', while ordinary MPs
are simply 'Honourable'. When referring to a Member of the same
party, an MP would call him or her 'my Honourable Friend'; if from
another party, 'the Honourable Gentleman/Lady'. If the Member is a
Queen's Counsel, he is a 'Learned Member', and if he has been a
serving member of the Armed Forces he is a 'Gallant Member'. If the
Member was a commissioned officer, he is 'Honourable and Gallant'.
This form of address can make for quite a mouthful at times. The
longest form is 'My Right Honourable, Learned and Gallant Friend,
the Member for X'. Although this language does appear to be archaic
and anachronistic, it certainly helps to prevent MPs being referred to
in an abusive or derogatory way in the heat of debate. 'You are an
idiot' would be far more likely to provoke an angry response than 'The
Honourable Member for X is behaving idiotically.'

Political Codewords

Tired and emotional	Drunk and disorderly
Courageous	Stupid and dangerous
Imaginative	Lunatic
With respect	You're talking a lot of nonsense
With great respect	You're talking an even bigger load of nonsense
With very great respect	You've clearly lost your marbles
Depressed regions	Marginal constituencies
Novel	Ridiculous
Frank and full discussion	An unholy row too libellous to print
In all honesty	Prepare to hear a pack of lies
A meteoric rise	And I hope they'll burn out soon
A formidable talent	An unbearable smart-alec
The master of his brief	The servant of his advisers

Speeches must be relevant and reasonably free from repetition. They must not include what is known as 'unparliamentary language' (those words and phrases that Speakers have ruled would lower the reputation of Parliament if used), and they should not refer to any trial that is pending or proceeding (*sub judice*) in case they should prejudice it. The Speaker often has to rule whether a certain word or phrase is unparliamentary. For example:

MR TONY BANKS: Is not the Chancellor of the Exchequer (Mr Nigel Lawson) insulting the House by refusing to come here and make a statement on what is clearly a matter of grave significance for the economy? Not only does the Right Hon. Gentleman physically resemble Nero, but he is clearly adopting the same attitude. Will you confirm, Mr Speaker, that you have the power to order the fat bounder to be dragged here from the dinner table?

MR SPEAKER: Order. First I have not that power. Secondly, I dislike that expression, which I ask the Honourable Gentleman to withdraw.

MR BANKS: In that case, Mr Speaker, I shall say 'the corpulent bounder'.
MR SPEAKER: That is almost as bad.

There is a ban on calling other Members liars. However, many Members have got round this objection by one means or another. Prime Minister Churchill used 'terminological inexactitude' for lie and got away with it. The cleverest was probably the playwright MP Richard Brinsley Sheridan, who, when pulled up for calling another Member a liar, replied, 'Mr Speaker, Sir, I said the Honourable Gentleman was a liar it is true and I am sorry for it.' He went on to say that the Honourable Member could put the punctuation marks where he liked. A more unusual case of unparliamentary language occurred when Speaker Weatherill used a word that, from any other Member, would certainly have been ruled to be unparliamentary! Also MPs may not make any criticism of the Royal Family or the judiciary. Erskine May, the encyclopaedia of parliamentary procedure, says, 'Unless the discussion is based on a substantive motion, reflections must not be cast upon the sovereign, the heir to the throne, or any of the Royal Family.'

Some of the most interesting cases of unparliamentary language are the insults which have been allowed: in November 1991, Labour leader Neil Kinnock called another Member a 'jerk' and, although he withdrew the comment, was not named or asked to leave the chamber. Prime Minister Margaret Thatcher in turn had called the Labour leader a 'crypto-communist' and got away with it in 1990.

It is up to the Speaker to determine whether Members' comments are unparliamentary. In Erskine May, under 'Allegations against Members', 'unparliamentary language is determined by its intent'. If the remark is slanderous or suggests that the subject has knowingly deceived the House, then it is ruled unparliamentary. That is why one Member cannot be called a liar, while another can be described as a jerk.

During the course of his or her speech, an MP may frequently be asked to 'give way' in order to let another Member make a point or ask a question. It is up to the MP who is speaking to decide whether or not to allow the intervention but convention dictates that he or she should usually give way. The number of MPs wishing to speak in the most popular debates has led to a ruling that the Speaker may decide that at certain times no speech should exceed ten minutes. This development is generally regarded favourably by MPs, particularly back-benchers, as it increases their chance of being called to speak. It does, however, limit the extent to which Members will 'give way', since they lose time from their ten-minute ration if they do so.

All MPs present in the chamber, as well as the MP actually speaking, must also behave in accordance with certain standards. Notes may be used, for example, but a speech should not be read, as it is considered impolite to lecture the House in that manner. Strictly speaking, it is not permitted for a Member to wander around the chamber, to read, hold a conversation or walk in front of an MP who is speaking. These rules are generally ignored in favour of common sense; during the course of a debate there is a fairly regular flow of MPs in and out of the chamber.

While Members no longer read newspapers or books in the chamber, it is acceptable for them to read Hansard *Reports* or Erskine May. Some Members even deal with their correspondence while in the chamber or carry on quiet private conversations with their neighbours.

Members must bow to the Speaker's chair when they enter and leave the chamber and they are not allowed to eat or drink in the chamber. Smoking has not been permitted since 1676, when a resolution was passed 'that no Member do presume to take tobacco in the gallery of the House or at a committee table'. This resolution must make parts of the Palace of Westminster the oldest 'No Smoking' zone in the country, and means that the chamber of the Commons is green in more than one sense!

When the Speaker rises from her chair, all Members must sit down. This is generally sufficient to ensure reasonable order, but sometimes a Member will try to defy the chair. During a heated debate Members might let their emotions get the better of them. The indiscipline of certain Members has become increasingly apparent over recent years. If Members refuse to obey the Speaker's request for order, they can be asked to leave the chamber and not return for the rest of the day. If they persist in their dissent, the Speaker has no choice but to 'name' the Member. She does this by rising and saying, 'I must name the Hon. Member for – [constituency] – [name], for disregarding the authority of the chair.' A Government minister will then move that the named Member be suspended from the House. This may be accepted unanimously; if not, a division will be held. If the Member will not leave the chamber voluntarily, the Serjeant at Arms will ask him or her to leave. The doorkeepers may have to be summoned to remove the MP physically and on one occasion the police were actually brought into the Chamber to take away a Member. Most recently, in 1993, Dennis Skinner was named by the Speaker for calling John Gummer 'this little squirt of a Minister' and refusing to withdraw the remark.

The first time that a Member is 'named', the suspension lasts for five days; the next time, for twenty days and, if he or she should be 'named' again, the suspension lasts until the House decides to allow the MP to return.

'Namings' are generally noisy, emotional occasions when the main aim of the Speaker is to calm down the House and bring it to order. Some 'namings' occur because of a Member's spontaneous words or actions, but some are deliberately planned by the Member involved. For example, it was known in advance that Jim Sillars was going to make a protest which might lead to his being 'named' just before the Chancellor made his Budget Statement on 14 March 1989 (see page 52).

Under the Jopling changes, the Speaker has wider discretion to limit back-bench speeches to ten minutes and front-benchers will strive to limit opening speeches to thirty minutes and their closing speeches to twenty. Under the old standing orders, the longest back-bench speech was four hours and twenty-three minutes by Sir Ivan Lawrence, opposing the Water (Fluoridation) Bill of 6 March 1985 (see also section on 'Fibustering' on p. 77).

The record for the longest speech in House of Commons history is held by the Rt Hon. Henry Peter Brougham (1778–1868), who, on 7 February 1828, spoke for six hours on law reform. Then he went on to secure the Lords record after being made first Lord Brougham and Vaux, on 7 October 1831, when he spoke on the second reading of the Reform Bill 'fortified by three tumblers of spiced wine'.

SUBSTANTIVE MOTIONS

Debates that do not involve legislation take two forms: substantive motions and adjournment motions (see page 72).

Substantive motions are those that express a particular opinion or viewpoint. The Government also initiates debates on substantive motions, concerning not just procedural matters but such subjects as financial assistance to Opposition parties (26 November 1987), Hong Kong (20 January 1988), the Inner London Education Authority (17 February 1988), the defence estimates (19 October 1988) and broadcasting and terrorism (2 November 1988). There are two annual debates on substantive motions in the Commons: on the Queen's Speech and on the Chancellor's Budget Speech.

OPPOSITION SUBSTANTIVE MOTIONS

The most common form of substantive motion occurs in the twenty Opposition days each session. These are days on which motions chosen by the Opposition parties are debated (seventeen of them are given to the official Opposition party). One example, on 1 February 1989, was when the House of Commons debated the following motion moved, or proposed, by Michael Meacher:

I beg to move that this House, noting that the number of low-paid workers below the European decency threshold has increased by two million since 1979 and that the lowest paid are now relatively poorer than at any time for a century, strongly condemns the Government's proposal to abolish the Wages Councils which will depress the living standards of millions of families and will encourage employers to compete by wage-cutting rather than by improved efficiency.

Norman Fowler, representing the Government, proposed the following amendment:

I beg to move, to leave out from 'House' to the end of the question and add instead thereof:

'noting that since the Government came to power personal disposable income has increased at every level in society and that the lowest paid have had proportionately higher increases than many other groups, considers that the best way in which the Government can help the low paid is by creating the conditions for more jobs by breaking down the barriers to employment and encouraging labour market flexibility; and welcomes the Government's decision to consult about the abolition of Wages Councils'.

NO CONFIDENCE MOTIONS

A particularly important form of Opposition-sponsored debate may be the one which moves that the House has 'no confidence' in the Government. If the Government majority is small or if it has no overall majority in the House, then the Opposition may try to have a No Confidence Motion passed. If such a motion is passed, then the Government is obliged to resign and call a general election. Obviously, therefore, the atmosphere in the House on these occasions is extremely tense. The present Government came to power after winning the general election that followed the previous Labour Government's defeat on a No Confidence Motion.

On 28 March 1979 the motion 'that this House has no confidence in Her Majesty's Government' was debated. At 10 p.m. the Speaker put the question and the division bells rang out to indicate that a vote was being taken. It was clear that the vote would be extremely close. The Government needed every vote it could get if it was to survive. Even in this time of high drama, farce intervened. The Independent MP for Fermanagh and South Tyrone, Frank Maguire, was not often to be found at Westminster. He had been elected in 1974 and when he died, in 1981, he still had not made his maiden speech. However, he had supported the Labour Government in some important votes before this No Confidence debate and again his vote was going to be crucial.

As Frank Maguire had followed a policy of near-abstention from Westminster, it was not even certain that he would attend the debate.

In the event, he did appear. How he would cast his vote was the subject of much discussion among MPs. When the result of the division was announced, the No Confidence Motion had been passed by one vote, 311 to 310. Frank Maguire had come 'to personally abstain' and by so doing he made an awesome contribution to the defeat of the Government.

WEDNESDAY MORNING ADJOURNMENT DEBATES

Before the Jopling changes, Private Members' non-legislative motions were debated on ten Fridays and four half-days each session. Since January 1995, however, with the exception of Private Members' bills, Private Members' business – that is, Private Members' motions and Consolidated Fund and some other adjournment debates – is taken during Wednesday morning sittings to avoid late-night sittings after 7 p.m. on a Thursday before a non-sitting Friday. Under the Jopling rules, therefore, Private Members' motions have been superseded by Wednesday morning adjournment debates.

The Members who introduce these motions are decided by ballot and the motion is of their choosing. The successful Members must give a minimum of nine days' notice of the motion they will be proposing. These motions are only rarely taken to a vote; their real purpose lies in allowing the Members to give the House an opportunity to discuss motions that are usually less party political than motions proposed by the Government and Opposition.

On the morning of Wednesday 12 July 1995, for example, subjects debated under a motion to adjourn the House were intensive care in London (introduced by the Conservative MP Roger Sims), nuclear waste (introduced by the Labour MP Clive Betts), foetal pain (introduced by the Liberal Democrat MP David Alton), taxation on gilts and bonds (introduced by the Conservative MP Tim Smith) and, finally, the therapeutic use of cannabis (introduced by the Labour MP Paul Flynn).

ADJOURNMENT MOTIONS

The second form of motion that does not relate to legislation is the adjournment motion, of which there are various types. The daily adjournment debate, which takes place after the day's business has been conducted, lasts thirty minutes. The motion to adjourn is moved by a Government Whip. A back-bencher then normally speaks for about fifteen minutes on a subject that he or she has given prior notice of and which must come within the responsibilities of the Government. In theory only one back-bencher speaks, but he or she may allow 'interventions' by other Members, generally by prior arrangement. This has the disadvantage of cutting into the allotted time, but the MP has the advantage of showing wider support for his or her views.

The relevant Minister replies for the remaining time allowed, normally fifteen minutes, and the House then adjourns without taking a vote. The choice of which back-bencher is allowed to speak is made by ballot, except on Thursday, when the Speaker is allowed to decide who may speak.

The subjects of the daily adjournment motions during one week (13–17 February 1989) were the future of the Barrow-in-Furness Crown Court; the tolls of the Severn Bridge; the bypass for the villages of Redberth and Sageston; the Rate Support Grant in Derbyshire; and planning appeals in Croydon. As can be seen, the matters covered are extraordinarily specific and of very limited interest. This, and the time of night, mean that most adjournment debates are carried out in an almost empty chamber. It is, nevertheless, a way of getting statements 'on the record'. It has, for example, been used by MPs to say things that, outside the House, would attract a libel suit.

The Government also sponsors adjournment debates; this may be because the Opposition cannot move an amendment to the motion 'that this House do now adjourn'. Thus, when a Government adjournment debate takes the form of a debate on a controversial aspect of Government policy, there is no real opportunity for Government rebels to defeat the Government.

Even if Government back-benchers do use the debate to criticize the Government, and vote with the Opposition, this rebellion has no effect on Government policy, because the motion being debated did not mention any actual policy.

This mechanism of adjournment motions may also be used to allow the House to express views on subjects for which the Government has no particular policy.

CONSOLIDATED FUND BILL

Every session there are three Consolidated Fund Bills and these arise from the Commons' function of scrutinizing expenditure. Basically, the Government presents supply estimates, the purpose of which is to ask for money to be supplied and to detail how it is to be spent. The Commons vote on the first supply estimate no later than 6 February, the second no later than 18 March and the third no later than 5 August.

Before the Jopling changes were implemented, a motion to adjourn the House was debated after the vote on each supply estimate on each Consolidated Fund Bill from that evening until 9 a.m. the following morning. Back-benchers wishing to speak on particular subjects in these debates entered their names in a ballot. Subjects that attracted the most interest were given three hours in which to be debated; only one and a half hours were granted for less popular subjects. Similar sorts of rule now apply to the Wednesday morning debates.

The fact that the Consolidated Fund debate used to take place throughout the night meant that, like other adjournment debates, attendance was often limited to the Deputy Speaker, the back-bencher, the Minister and the Whip. It is best characterized by the following possibly apocryphal exchange between the policeman at the door and a Member arriving to speak at 4 a.m.:

POLICEMAN: Good morning, Sir.
MP: Good morning. I am hoping to speak in the debate.
POLICEMAN: Very good, Sir. Will it make any difference?

Of course, very often it did not. On the other hand, some of the earliest shots in a successful campaign were fired in a Consolidated Fund Bill debate (see, for example, Chapter 12).

STANDING ORDER NO. 20

The last type of adjournment motion is that applied for under Standing Order No. 20 (SO No. 20) – the emergency adjournment debate for which twenty-four hours' notice is usually required. Applications for emergency debates are now fairly infrequent. The Speaker will not hear an application which falls well short of the criteria in the Standing Order.

To grant an emergency debate, the Speaker must feel that the issue is of national importance and is unlikely to be debated by some other means. In the 1984–5 session, for example, MPs made sixty-one applications for debates under SO No. 20 but only one was granted, and during the 1992–93 session, only nineteen applications were made.

Although MPs do not expect their applications to receive debate, this SO No. 20 procedure is of benefit to them in that it allows them three minutes to state why they feel an emergency debate is necessary. A successful application for a debate under SO No. 20 was granted on 12 April 1988 and debated the following day:

MR SPEAKER: I have received an enormous number of applications from Hon. Members on both sides of the House to take part in the debate. It would be extremely helpful if both front-bench speakers would make brief speeches and if the backbenchers would confine their speech to five minutes. There is hardly a constituency that is not affected by the changes one way or another. It is my wish that most of those who want to take part in the debate should be able to do so.

MR ROBIN COOK: I beg to move that this House do now adjourn. Today we are debating the impact of the social security changes that have been phased in over the past fortnight. The Government claim that these changes represent the biggest upheaval since the Government came to power, but I would not want it to be thought that this Government have been idle over the past nine years. In that time they have abolished the link between pensions and earnings, which means that the pension for a married couple is £14 less than it would otherwise be.

DIVISIONS

Votes in Parliament are known as divisions, because the Members cast their votes by physically dividing into two groups. At the end of a debate the Speaker 'puts the question'. In other words, she asks the House to come to a decision on the matter being debated. If the subject is entirely uncontroversial, she may hear only the Government Whips shout 'aye' and the question will be carried without a division. If, however, she hears shouts of both 'aye' and 'no', then the Speaker will say, according to which side she thinks is shouting loudest, 'I think the ayes/noes have it.' If there is further shouting, she announces that a vote will be taken by saying, 'Clear the lobby.'

Division bells begin to ring all over the Palace of Westminster and also in restaurants, pubs and MPs' homes that are close to the Houses of Parliament. MPs can be seen hurrying towards the chamber to vote as they have only eight minutes to get there. To register their vote they must enter the 'aye' or the 'no' division lobby (according to how they wish to vote) and these are on opposite sides of the chamber. Eight minutes after the division bells began to ring, the doors to the division lobbies are locked. The MPs are counted as they pass out of the lobbies and their votes are recorded by clerks. When all the MPs in the division lobbies have registered their votes, the result is given to the Speaker. The record number of divisions in one day is sixty-four from 23–24 March 1971, including fifty-seven in succession between midnight and noon. The largest majority on a division was 547 (556 for and nine against) on, you will find this hard to believe, a procedural motion relating to the European Communities (Amendment) Bill on 15 April 1994. So there is agreement on Europe after all!

If Members are ill, it is not necessary for them to walk through the lobbies to vote, but they have to be within the precincts of the palace for their vote to be registered. Lord Melbourne's Government in the 1830s once depended for its survival on the doctor of the House deciding that a Member was still breathing at the time of a division. Seriously ill Members have been brought to the palace to record their votes, to help maintain the Government's majority. One Member was actually brought all the way from Edinburgh.

In the event of a tied vote, the Speaker has a casting vote. She is obliged to vote in such a way as to allow the Commons to look at the issue again – that is, generally in favour of the *status quo*. There was one famous occurrence of a seventeenth-century Speaker who voted for an adjournment 'because he was hungry'!

POINTS OF ORDER

During debates MPs quite frequently make points of order. Technically these should be matters for the Speaker, about how the chamber is being run and how people are behaving within it. More often than not they are simply a way of drawing attention to something, and the point of order is chosen because the Speaker has to give priority to it once questions are over. Accordingly there is often a flurry of bogus points of order at the beginning of main business.

If a Member wishes to make a point of order when a division is taking place, he or she must speak sitting down and wearing a hat. Collapsible top hats are now kept in the chamber by the Serjeant at Arms. If a Member wishes to make a point of order during a division, one of these is skimmed along so that he or she may put it on and make the point.

PAIRING

When the Whips have issued a Three Line Whip (see page 142), the subject is extremely important and MPs are expected to vote. If only a One Line or Two Line Whip is issued for a vote, then MPs may 'pair' with each other. This means that two MPs – one from the Government party and one from the Opposition parties – agree not to vote in that division and so it is not necessary for either of them to attend the debate. The MPs involved have to let their party Whips know about their arrangements.

FILIBUSTERING

The best-known form of obstructing the business of Parliament is the filibuster, whereby a Member tries to 'talk out' a bill by discoursing for as long as possible in order to take up so much time that the measure being debated cannot receive adequate consideration. Henry Brougham was a master of the filibuster in the nineteenth century, having set records for the longest speeches in the chambers of both Houses. As Lord Brougham he spoke in the Lords, for six hours, during the second reading of the Reform Bill 1831. One of his biographers, in *Anecdotal History of the British Parliament*, described the speech in the House of Lords thus:

It certainly was a wonderful performance to witness. He showed a most stupendous memory, and extraordinary dexterity in handling the weapons both of ridicule and of reason ... The peroration was partly inspired by draughts of mulled port, imbibed by him very copiously.

However, even Lord Brougham would probably have been surprised at the length of the speech delivered by Labour MP John Golding, during the committee stage of the British Telecommunications Bill 1983. He spoke for an incredible eleven and a quarter hours, between

6.07 p.m. on Tuesday 8 February and 5.22 a.m. on Wednesday 9 February 1983.

This was no mean achievement, considering that all speeches have to be relevant and fairly unrepetitive. Just imagine how long John Golding could have spoken if he did not have to stick to these rules!

The Speaker may, on occasion, use his or her discretion to impose a Ten Minute Rule during a debate, limiting the time a Member can speak to ten minutes.

CLOSURE

In 1880–81 Charles Stewart Parnell, leader of the Irish parliamentary party, conducted a deliberate policy of obstructing parliamentary business and, as a direct response to this tactic, the closure was introduced in 1881. What happens is that, after a measure has been debated for some time, an MP can rise and say, 'I beg to move that the question be now put.' If a Speaker feels that sufficient time has already been spent debating the matter, he or she then allows the Closure Motion to be voted upon without debate. If it is passed, and provided also that at least 100 members voted for it, then the House immediately votes on the 'original question' – that is, the question that was being debated before the Closure Motion was moved.

GUILLOTINES

An extension of the closure procedure is that of 'closure by compartments' or the 'guillotine'. This is a device that is used to set a time limit on the discussion of a bill. Again, this measure was principally inspired by the obstructionist tactics of Parnell's party. In 1887, the House decided to guillotine discussion on the Criminal Law Amendment (Ireland) Bill. This Bill had been debated for an incredible thirty-five days before the guillotine was introduced. The minister responsible for the bill described the use of the guillotine in this instance as

> absolutely essential in the interests of the honour and dignity of Parliament and the duties which are imposed upon the Members of the House of Commons ... We have arrived at the fourth month of the session and we have practically done nothing except to consider the measure now before the House ... The whole course of legislation has been stopped.

So, while the guillotine was originally something of an emergency measure, it is now used more frequently. The timetable for discussion of a bill is laid down before the House in the form of a motion which is debated for three hours. If the motion is agreed to, then all consideration of the bill simply ends on the specified date, regardless of whether all the clauses of the bill have been discussed.

Although the use of the guillotine is often controversial, it is essential if Parliament is to be able to conduct its business. Clement Attlee remarked that 'democracy means Government by discussion, but it is only effective if you can stop people talking'. According to Michael Foot, ex-leader of the Labour Party, all is fair in love, war and parliamentary procedure!

Another factor that limits debates is the Speaker's power to select a number of representative amendments to legislation or motions, rather than having all amendments discussed. This device used to be known as the 'kangaroo', and was first used on the discussion of the Finance Bill 1909.

QUORUM

A quorum is no longer necessary for debate to proceed in the House of Commons. Until 1971, if there were fewer than forty Members in the chamber, an MP could rise and bring this fact to the Speaker's attention. The Speaker would then say, 'Notice having been taken that forty Members are not present, strangers will withdraw.' The division bells would ring and, unless forty Members were in the chamber at the end of eight minutes, the House would immediately adjourn.

In the years before this rule was abolished, a passing reference during a speech remarking upon the number of Members present would have constituted a call for a quorum. In the days when only two minutes were given for Members to get into the chamber before the count was made, this rule was more rigidly applied. Sir Reginald Palgrave recounted the story of a Member who managed to count himself out. He was a rather boring orator and so only a few Members were present on one occasion when he was speaking. According to Sir Reginald, because he was displeased by the poor attendance:

He joked about the crowded benches, the packed House, that he pretended to see around. The jest was fatal, he had referred to the number present; this done, the Speaker must determine what the number is. 'Order! Order!' from the chair, silenced the debater. Amazed, he sat down, quite ignorant of the effect of his wit – the Speaker rose in all solemnity, in due custom he began the regular, 'One, two, three', as his extended arm pointed in stately circuit to each Member. Soon all was over; the two minutes elapsed but twenty heads were counted and the House broke up, much in laughter at the luckless orator, who had counted himself out.

Although the practice of counting out has been ended, a quorum of forty is still necessary today for the business of the House to proceed. If fewer than forty Members participate in a division, that business must be held over until the next sitting of the House, and the House passes on to the next matter.

THE HOUSE OF LORDS

Debates in the House of Lords are altogether far gentler than in the Commons. Partly this is as a result of the absence of the pressure of the ballot box – members of the Upper House do not need to catch the headlines to retain their seats. Partly, however, this courtly style is necessary in a chamber whose equivalent of the Speaker has virtually no authority. There are many symptoms of this difference: no closures, no time limitations of any sort, almost no limit on amendments at committee, report and third reading, no limit on supplementary questions and no casting vote in the event of a tie. Even the lobbies reflect the serenity of the Lords; instead of 'aye' and 'no' lobbies, they have 'content' and 'not content'. It is self-policing in a peculiarly British way. While there is party conflict, it is almost always courteous conflict. Were it not so, one suspects that the system would collapse and the House of Lords as we know it would be reformed into a different being altogether.

6

HOW GOVERNMENT MAKES LAWS

Law is made in Parliament by considering bills. Once a bill has received Royal Assent it becomes law – an Act of Parliament. Bills can be introduced in either House.

POLICY FORMULATION

The creation of new policies is a complex and variable business. Political parties decide by a variety of processes what their policies will be. They are then put into a manifesto so that the electorate can consider them. If the party obtains a majority of seats in a general election it will form a Government and set about implementing most or all of its manifesto commitments. Once in Government, new policies may arise from Civil Service proposals on specific problem areas or they may be created as a result of new initiatives by party or near-party groups. In the case of a Conservative Government this may include bodies such as the Adam Smith Institute, the Centre for Policy Studies or the Institute of Economic Affairs. The Labour Party might adopt ideas from the Fabian Society or those promoted by Tribune and so on. In some cases, bills are introduced because of concerted pressure from special interest groups. For example, the work of the Royal Society for the Prevention of Cruelty to Animals (RSPCA) has led to tighter controls on animal welfare.

Urgent problems may lead to new laws. The Firearms Amendment Bill became law after the Home Secretary responded to public pressure which was a direct result of a mad gunman perpetrating a massacre in Hungerford in 1987.

An essential element of the Government's decision as to which bills to promote during each session is the length and complexity of the proposed legislation. In this respect, the Leader of the House and the Chief Whip have to give careful consideration to the time that each measure will take to pass through Parliament.

THE FLGS AND THE LGS

Every year the Government has to decide which legislation to introduce in the following session, starting in November, and therefore to announce in the Queen's Speech. This is done by the legislative committee of the Cabinet. The workings of this committee and its composition were shrouded in secrecy. However, the membership and terms of reference of the Ministerial Committees on the Queen's Speeches and Future Legislation (FLG) and on Legislation (LG) are now published.

Once the FLGs have made recommendations to the Cabinet, the general scheme of the legislative programme is delegated to the relevant minister. The minister and his or her department deal with the nuts and bolts of a proposed bill. Civil servants advise the minister and a detailed scheme of the proposed legislation is drawn up and submitted to the Cabinet.

GREEN AND WHITE PAPERS

Most new law is created after a fairly formal process of consultation. Once implemented, law is hard to change, so it is important that it should be right first time.

The first stage of the governmental process is often the publication of a Green Paper. This consultative document is designed to provoke responses from interested parties that might be affected by the proposals. These responses are considered by the department involved, and they influence the final policy proposals, which are agreed by the Prime Minister and probably the full Cabinet. The proposals will then be published as a White Paper, which is essentially a statement of Government intentions. The Home Secretary, for example, introduced a Green Paper after the Southall riots in 1979. This led in 1985 to a White Paper called *The Review of Public Order* and was followed by the introduction of the Public Order Bill 1986.

The timing and organization of this procedure are dictated by events and the nature of the issue. Where legislation needs to be quickly implemented, a White Paper might be published only the day before it is first introduced into the House.

PARLIAMENTARY DRAFTSMEN

Once a bill has Cabinet approval it needs to be drafted in a legal form. The Cabinet Committee or the department involved sends a Memorandum of Instruction to the lawyers – Parliamentary Counsel – to do this. Parliamentary Counsel are instructed by the solicitors in the appropriate department. As the law will have to be interpreted by lawyers and ultimately by the courts, it should be drafted in clear legal terms. The solicitors and barristers of the Parliamentary Counsel are experienced in this, but even so several versions are often necessary before the final form is ready. The final draft is examined by a law officer of the Crown and also by the LG before being presented to Parliament.

ALLOCATION OF TIME

In the Queen's Speech, the Government first states publicly what major legislation it is proposing that session. In November 1994, the Queen announced that the Government would, amongst other things, introduce Bills to equalize the state pension age between men and women, to improve the management of the National Health Service, to privatize the commercial activities of the Atomic Energy Authority, and to reform the Scottish criminal justice system. The endless stream of

demands for legislation was described in a speech to the House by
Herbert Asquith in 1912:

I do not exaggerate when I say that if you were to sit continuously during the
whole twelve months of the year, and worked through them with unremitting
ardour and assiduity, you would find at the end not only that there were still
large arrears of legislation which you had not even attempted to undertake,
not only enormous sums raised by taxation whose appropriation had never
even been discussed, but that there were vast areas of the Empire . . . to whose
concerns we had not been able to devote so much as one single night.

The situation today is very much worse than it was in his day.
Parliament meets for longer, both in hours per day and days per year,
in fact longer today than any other democratic parliament its size.
Legislation is more complex, and MPs have to be much more professional in response to outside pressures.

THE FIRST READING

A bill can be introduced following an order of the House or it can be
presented by a minister or any other Member without an order. Having
been presented (or, in the case of a bill brought from the Lords, having
been taken up by a minister or other Members), it is given a first
reading without a motion or a debate. Each Government bill has to
be introduced by the minister responsible or another minister on his
or her behalf. The Health and Medicines Bill, for example, was presented to the House of Commons on 25 November 1988 by the then
Minister of State for Health, Tony Newton.

A bill receives its First Reading when the clerk of the House reads
its short title. The motion that the bill be given a first reading is carried
without discussion and this indeed was the case with the Health and
Medicines Bill. The bill is then printed and made available to Members
for consideration prior to the second reading. Before printing was
invented, bills were read out in full by the clerk, and this practice
continued well into the eighteenth century. Indeed, this was a necessity

in the days when the ability to read was uncommon, and the clerk of the House was therefore chosen principally for this ability.

THE SECOND READING

'Politics are almost as exciting as war and quite as dangerous. In war you can only be killed once, but in politics many times.' *Sir Winston Churchill*

'I hardly ever had to make an important speech without feeling violently sick most of the day before.' *Harold Macmillan*

The bill then proceeds to the second reading, which it normally receives two or three weeks later. There should be at least two weekends between first reading and second reading for proper deliberation even for relatively rapid legislation, such as the Dock Work Bill 1989.

The second reading is the occasion for major debate on the principles of the bill. Usually this lasts for one day, and a minor bill may take only half a day. Very few bills are given more than one day. Government bills are very rarely defeated on second reading – one such case since the present Government came to power in 1979 was the Shops Bill in April 1986. Only three second reading votes have been lost by a Government this century.

If a bill passes this stage of the law-making process, it means that the House accepts it in principle: 'I beg to move that the bill be now read a second time.'

The second reading is the first point at which the Government seeks approval of Parliament, and so lobby groups take this opportunity to try and sway the opinions of MPs. It is therefore the first time that the Government hears MPs' attitudes to the bill expressed openly, although the Whips may have pre-warned the Government of the general feeling of MPs, having done their soundings and calculations before the debate starts.

Generally the second reading is considered a battle between the Opposition and the Government, with the Whips ensuring that the Government MPs support the minister. However, this is not always so. The Health and Medicines Bill proved to be contentious and Government back-benchers voiced their criticism. Dame Jill Knight was one such dissident:

May I start by saying, wistfully, that I would like to be able to support this bill. The bill contains some things that are right. I must also tell the minister that a significant number of our Honourable Members are anxious about the proposals in the bill. There is no doubt that there is also a large body of concern among the citizens outside the House.

Others were more pointed. Jerry Hayes, a forthright Conservative MP who led the 'rebellion' on this bill, was particularly annoyed that charges for eyesight tests and dental check-ups had been inserted since the publication of the White Paper. Disappointment was all the greater for this 'rebellious group' since the White Paper, *Promoting Better Health*, had been enormously popular.

Bills are defeated at this stage by moving an amendment to the original question put at the start of a second reading 'that the Bill be now read a second time', or simply by voting down the original question.

To follow this example through, the Health and Medicines Bill passed its second reading easily, because most of its provisions were concerned solely with creating a better system of primary health care. These provisions were very popular with Government back-benchers. This was not the time to challenge the unpopular parts – charging for eyesight and dental tests. That challenge would come at a later stage.

In former times it was not unknown to tear up the bill when it was officially rejected, as was reported in the twentieth edition of Erskine May:

On 23 January 1562, a bill was rejected and ordered to be torn; so, also, on the 17 March 1620, Sir Edward Coke moved 'to have the bill torn in the House'; and is entered that the bill was accordingly 'rejected and torn, without one negative'. Even so late as 3 June 1772 the Lords having amended a money clause in the Corn Bill, Governor Pownall moved that the bill be rejected, and the Speaker, according to his promise, threw it over the table, 'several members on both sides of the House kicking it as they went out'.

In modern times the treatment of rejected bills is less dramatic.

THE COMMITTEE STAGE

Having successfully passed through its second reading, a bill undergoes a detailed examination in standing committee. Here clauses are debated and amendments voted upon. Eighteen Members were allocated to Standing Committee A, to consider the Health and Medicines Bill. The Members of a standing committee often invite specialist advisers to attend the committee sessions, and these advisers may offer their host MP advice in the corridor.

Once in committee, a Member may really make his or her influence felt on a bill, because party political divides are not always clearly defined. Ministers can rely on their civil servants attending the committee to back them up, but their back-benchers are free to criticize.

The minister responsible for the bill has to steer it through the committee sessions in person. Since the principle of a bill has, at this stage, already been accepted, the committee restricts itself to considering it clause by clause and amendments are put forward on points of detail. This can lead to elongated discussions, delaying tactics and misuse of parliamentary time. Nicholas Baker, MP, remarked in 1984 that 'too often these committees turn into a form of trench warfare'. Once the committee has finished discussing a bill, successful amendments are inserted and then printed and circulated.

For the Health and Medicines Bill, the committee stage was where the real fight began. The objection of the rebels was to a particular set of clauses, not to the principle of the whole bill, so this was the appropriate time and place to argue it out. The most dramatic moment came when Jerry Hayes made his speech on 11 February 1988:

I have now expressed my views and those of professional bodies. I shall now quote what ministers have said.

During the second reading of the Health and Social Security Bill on 20 December 1983, the then Secretary of State for Social Services, my Right Hon. Friend the Member for Sutton Coldfield (Mr Norman Fowler), said: 'We believe that the access to a free sight test is important in detecting serious eye disease.'

My Right Hon. Friend is still in the Cabinet: he is now Secretary of State for Employment.

In the same debate, the then Minister for Health, my Right Hon. and Learned Friend, the Member for Rushcliffe (Mr Kenneth Clarke), who is still in the Cabinet and is now Chancellor of the Duchy of Lancaster, declared: 'We are keeping in the NHS what should be kept there – free sight tests for everyone, regardless of need. That is the major health element that the NHS provides.'

The same Minister stated: 'It is essential that the NHS provide properly for the health needs of the population, and the NHS will continue to provide a sight test for everyone regardless of age or means.'

I have a letter from the Prime Minister dated 30 June 1980. It is on Downing Street notepaper and is addressed to a Mr G. Douglas. My Right Hon. Friend writes:

'Dear Mr Douglas,

'Thank you for your letter of 24 April about the proposed introduction of a charge for sight-tests in the General Ophthalmic Service (GOS). I am sorry that I have not been able to send you an earlier reply.

'As you may already know, the Government have decided to drop the proposal in response to strong representations that such a charge, in a service which has a preventive function, would be wrong in principle and could deter patients from seeking professional advice. We are currently examining ways of raising the revenue by other means within the GOS and an announcement will be made in due course.'

That is what the Prime Minister said in writing on 23 June 1980 – the same argument as I am presenting. That is also what the Minister and the Secretary of State for Health said not ten or fifteen years ago but in 1983 and 1984. That must be significant. I await with interest the comments of the Ministers.

The effect on the Committee was stunning. There was a sharp intake of breath on the Conservative side – and glee on the Labour benches.

Jerry Hayes *had* warned the ministers that he had something serious to bring up. He had not said what and he had not told the department Whip. The resulting discussion between the Whip and Hayes in the corridor outside the committee room was, in Hayes's own words, 'brisk and lively'.

SPECIAL STANDING COMMITTEES

Since 1981 a total of six bills has been considered by what are known as special standing committees. They differ from standing committees in that, before the clause-by-clause deliberation of the bill begins, the committee can meet for up to four sessions, as a select committee, to hear evidence from expert witnesses on the bill's provisions. Three of the four sittings are for hearing evidence; the first is for deciding what evidence to hear. This method has not yet been used often, but it undoubtedly enables the committee to go on to consider the bill in detail with some previous knowledge of the issues involved.

THE REPORT STAGE

After the amendments accepted by the standing committee have been printed, the chairman or woman of the standing committee reports the bill as amended to the House at the end of the committee stage. This is known as the report stage, or the 'consideration stage'. A debate follows as to whether or not the amendments should be accepted and whether further amendments should be made. Then the bill is reprinted with all the amendments made in committee.

Because of the large number of amendments that will usually have been tabled, not all can be debated at the report stage. It is up to the Speaker to decide which are discussed. If time was short in committee, members of the committee might propose amendments that would otherwise have been discussed there. Alternatively, the minister may well have promised to discuss certain amendments at this stage, before the House. It is possible for the report stage itself to be taken into committee, but this has happened only once, in the case of the Water Resources Bill 1968.

If battle over the Health and Medicines Bill commenced at the committee stage, war broke out at report stage. Jill Knight and Jerry Hayes had written to all Conservative backbenchers stating their case

– which proved persuasive for a significant number. Indeed, about sixty Members signed an Early Day Motion supporting their objections. Such a parliamentary petition is a public commitment on the part of the signatories to a certain stance – in this case against charges for eye tests and dental check-ups – and it can be construed as throwing down the gauntlet. In this instance, the rebels' challenge was accepted by the Government. In theory, sixty Government Members changing their vote will convert a winning majority of 100 to a losing one of twenty. The Whips went into action.

Everybody who signed the Early Day Motion was talked to, as well as others who expressed doubts. They were argued with, they were cajoled, they were given meetings with ministers. Most importantly, it was determined how they would vote – whether they would oppose or abstain. Part of the process was described by Colin Brown in the *Independent*, from the perspective of a 'new boy':

[He] voted against the Government over the introduction of charges for eye tests. There was intense pressure on him to back down. He was called to a meeting with Tony Newton, the Minister for Health; a second meeting with David Lightbown, his regional Whip; and a third meeting with John Moore, the Secretary of State, Mr Newton, Edwina Currie, the Parliamentary Under-Secretary, and officials.

'I came to the conclusion that the Government might be right, but the consequences of being wrong were irreversible,' he said. 'Everybody I met the following weekend in the constituency was very supportive, which surprised me. They said it was the right thing to do ... What impressed me was that there was a real process of consultation [from the Government]. I was the shop steward for my constituents. I suspect it would have been much tougher on me if the risk had been greater, had the Government been defeated. If I do it every day, I devalue my own currency. One of the reasons I got treated very reasonably is people know I would not do it lightly ... I was worrying about voting against the Government right up until the vote. I worried about it until the Minister sat down.'

Despite a conciliatory statement by the minister in charge of the bill, there occurred the expected rebellion of Government backbenchers.

However, the Government were not defeated on this bill at its report stage; the Government Whips had fulfilled their responsibility and many rebels had abstained rather than vote against the bill. In part this was because the minister announced that he was extending the number of people who qualified for free tests by 750,000, with special consideration for relatives of glaucoma sufferers. This was a significant achievement for the rebels. It now remained for the bill to be taken to the House of Lords. A number of the rebels had calculated early on that a Government victory at report stage was inevitable, so they were pinning their hopes of further change on a successful Lords' amendment that might then be accepted by the Government.

THE THIRD READING

The final stage of consideration of any proposed legislation is the third reading. This tends to be a formality. Third reading debates are almost always brief, but there have been some occasions when the debate is fierce. The last time a bill was defeated on third reading in the House of Commons was the Local Authority Works (Scotland) Bill 1977. Defeat at this stage for the Health and Medicines Bill was not a probability, nor indeed was it the intent of the rebels, since so much of the bill was so popular with the rebel camp itself.

LORDS' AMENDMENTS

The main function of the Lords is to review the bills from the Commons and to modify legislation. Also those clauses that were not debated in the House of Commons are considered in the Lords. As in the Commons, the bill is passed through the same process, starting with the first reading. The Chief Whip or another Government Whip presents the bill for the first reading, which is a formality. There are, however, some differences in the legislative process in the Lords. For example, if a bill in the Lords passes through to the committee stage, it normally goes before a committee of the whole House. It may, sometimes, be put before a select committee or a joint committee of both Houses. There is no guillotine procedure in the Lords, but fortunately filibusters are rare. Also amendments can be made in the Lords during the third reading debate.

Amendments to the Bill are printed in the name of the peers who are proposing them. All proposed amendments are inserted into the bill, which is then published. If no amendments are proposed, a date is suggested for the third reading or a postponement of the report stage is advised so that there is still an opportunity to amend the bill. All or part of the bill may be reconsidered by the committee of the whole House at any time between the committee stage and the third reading, so that the bill is thoroughly reviewed.

To return to our continuing saga of the Health and Medicines Bill. As the Commons rebels had hoped, the Lords did amend the bill to eliminate eye-test and dental charges. In this they were much influenced by the fact that every single back-bench speaker in the Commons debate spoke against the charges. This, however, was a combination of procedural coincidence and oversight by the Government.

In any controversial debate there is a tendency for the critics to be more vehement than the supporters, and therefore make a more determined effort to speak. It would have been quite easy to get a supporter of the Government's position (there were many) to make a very cogent defence of that position. Lack of planning and sheer luck went the other way, however, and so the Lords supported the rebels. As a result the bill was returned to the Commons to 'consider Lords' amendments'.

The battle really began to heat up even further. The Lords' amendment of the Health and Medicines Bill swung some doubters on to the rebel side – the Government might possibly be defeated. Nevertheless, at numerous meetings the then newly appointed Secretary of State for Health, Kenneth Clarke, made it clear to the backbenchers that he was not going to change his stance.

Since the election of the Conservative Government in 1979, there have been well over 100 Government defeats in the Lords. As a rule these defeats have served to amend bills, and in most cases the Government has accepted those amendments. (Sometimes the changes were dramatic. One Lords' amendment, for example, abolished corporal punishment in schools and thus effectively destroyed the Education [Corporal Punishment] Bill, which would have made corporal punishment conditional on parental consent.)

Each back-bencher did his or her own calculations. The Whips did their usual rounds, arguing, cajoling and counting. A new factor came into play. Long-term opponents of the then Prime Minister, Mrs Thatcher, on the Conservative back benches began to sense the possibility of defeating her.

The complexion of the rebellion began to change. Until this point it had not been a left- versus right-wing issue. Dame Jill Knight, for example, is on the right of the Conservative Party and was a leader of the rebellion. Now that the rebellion was beginning to become a left-wing one, some of the loyalists began to feel uncomfortable in such company and to look for compromises.

The day for debate arrived. The Whips and ministers were nervous but determined. At the very last minute – literally in the division lobby behind the chamber, as the debate got under way – one back-bencher struck a deal with the minister on enhancing the standards of eye tests. One more vote switched. The Secretary of State for Health, Mr Kenneth Clarke, made a typically combative opening speech. The debate continued in a heated manner, with highly effective performances from Opposition and Government Members. The mistake of the report stage was not repeated – there were plenty of Government back-benchers supporting the Government case this time. The ferocity of the argument continued right up until the last minute of the debate on dental charges. Nevertheless, the vote was won by the Government, 300 to 284. Some Conservative rebels resented the lack of turn-out from the Opposition parties – one Liberal MP was asleep in his office and Labour had a less than 100 per cent turn-out – but the battle was over. There was some suggestion that the Lords might reject the bill again, but there are, rightly, limits to the powers of an unelected Upper House. The Government had won the day.

Some bills pass through the House of Lords without any debate at all – for example, the Parliamentary Control of Expenditure (Reform) Bill 1983. On 9 May 1983 the Prime Minister announced that Parliament would be dissolved on 13 May and the general election held on 9 June. The Government was persuaded to take over this bill and it passed through the report and third reading with no amendment and no debate. Royal Assent was announced on 13 May, immediately before Parliament was dissolved.

When a bill has gone through all the stages and amendments have been made, it is sent back to the House of Commons. After both Houses have agreed on identical versions of a bill it is ready to receive Royal Assent. However, if the Commons disagree with the Lords' amendments, a committee sits to compile the reasons for the disagreement. The report is communicated to the Lords and, if they are insistent upon their amendments, the Commons continue with their consideration. The spirit of compromise normally wins the day and usually one or other of the Houses concedes.

THE POWER OF THE LORDS

The power of the Lords to prevent bills becoming law has been curbed and many would say that this has enabled the Upper House to survive. The Parliament Act 1911 states that the Lords must automatically accept purely financial legislation passed by the Commons. Such financial legislation can thus become law within one month of its passage through the Commons without the Lords' consent. In 1949 another Parliament Act was accepted with the result that any bill approved by the Commons twice in succession, in separate sessions with a year's interval, can become law without the consent of the Lords. In effect, this gives the Lords the ability to delay legislation by up to thirteen months – which, if a general election is in the offing, can be very significant.

ROYAL ASSENT

Royal Assent to a bill is given by the Norman French phrase *La Reyne le veult* (the Queen wishes it). The bill then becomes an Act of Parliament and has full legal authority. Royal Assent has not been given by the monarch in person since 1854 and it is now provided by Lords Commissioners on behalf of the monarch. It has not been refused since 1707, when Queen Anne withheld her consent to a Scottish Militia Bill.

HYBRID BILLS

Hybrid bills are public bills that have some of the characteristics of private bills (see Chapter 7). A hybrid bill was described by Speaker Hylton-Foster as 'a public bill which affects a particular private interest in a manner different from the private interests of other persons or bodies of the same category or class'.

If the clerks in the Public Bill Office decide that a particular bill is in fact a hybrid bill, it is referred to the Examiners of Petitions for Private Bills. The bill cannot receive its second reading until the examiners have reported on whether the standing orders on private business have been complied with. Once the second reading has been completed, the bill goes before a select committee (the members of which are chosen partly by the House and partly by the committee of selection).

If a hybrid bill is petitioned against, it is considered by a select committee. It is then recommitted and thereafter proceeds as a public bill. If no petitions are deposited, the select committee is discharged. The report stage and the third reading of a hybrid bill are the same as for public bills. It then goes to the House of Lords, and, if it is accepted by the Lords, it receives Royal Assent. The Channel Tunnel Rail Link Act 1987/8 began life as a hybrid bill.

STATUTORY INSTRUMENTS

A major bill is very complex and the schemes that are necessary to give effect to the law are so detailed that Parliament cannot hope to consider all the various requirements of each bill. Therefore it can give an enabling power to the relevant secretary of state to introduce a detailed scheme at a later date.

When the Government is ready to introduce this detailed scheme, the minister has to present a draft statutory instrument into Parliament. Statutory instruments, along with orders in council and the bylaws of local authorities and public corporations, are known as secondary or 'delegated' legislation. The rules used by the Department of Social Security and the Department for Education and Employment to flesh out the recent Jobseekers Allowance Act – details on eligibility for benefit, or on the level of allowance, for example – were presented to Parliament as Statutory Instruments.

So-called 'affirmative' instruments have to be approved before they come into force (or within a specified period after coming into force), whereas 'negative' instruments come into force unless either House votes against them. Much delegated legislation is not subject to either form of parliamentary control.

EUROPEAN UNION DIRECTIVES

As a result of the UK joining the European Community (EC) in 1973, the power to make law has been supplemented by the European Communities Act 1972, the European Communities (Amendment) Act 1986 (also known as the Single European Act) and the European Communities (Amendment) Act 1993 (on the Maastricht treaty). The power to make law in certain European matters has been transferred from the British Parliament to the Council of Ministers. Every Wednesday a European standing committee meets to discuss all matters relating to the European Union.

European parliamentary laws are made by way of regulations and directives. Regulations must be implemented by the country they are addressed to without any amendment. An EU directive, on the other hand, sets down objectives that the European Union wishes to achieve and, although the country to which it is addressed must introduce a directive by the last date specified, it is at the country's discretion as to how they implement it and give effect to it.

The majority of European legislation is made through directives and therefore Parliament has the ability to make appropriate legislation in this respect. However, in all areas affected by directives and regulations, Parliament is no longer sovereign in that the European Union has power over and above the British Parliament. Until 1986 individual countries could veto European proposals in the Council of Ministers. This meant that the loss of sovereignty was nominal. Since the passing of the Single European Act, however, the right to veto has been severely reduced, although the national parliament does still retain formal supremacy and sovereignty, because it has the power to repeal the European Communities Act 1972.

CONCLUSION

The role of Parliament in the making of law is not just to provide rubber-stamp approval, even when the Government has a large majority. The use of tactical procedures, good debating and well-orchestrated arguments to contest a bill can cause a Government to change substantially its original plans. Furthermore, Members of both Houses continually have the opportunity of introducing changes to the law. Parliament is, therefore, in a very real sense, the final determiner of law.

7

PRIVATE MEMBERS' BILLS AND PRIVATE LEGISLATION

Private legislation is carried out not by the Government but by individual MPs, while Private Members' Bills are considered public legislation.

PRIVATE MEMBERS' BILLS

Private Members' business may consist of Private Members' Bills or non-legislative motions for debates selected by ballots. When there is no determined opposition to a Private Member's Bill, the first half-dozen in a parliamentary session have some hope of reaching the statute book.

Before the Jopling changes, Private Members' business mainly took place on a Friday when, because of restricted time, filibustering – or 'talking out' a bill – was common and highly effective. Private Members' business is now also debated on Wednesday mornings, and strict time limits on debates have been introduced to curb filibustering and its interference with business on Friday. During the Jopling experiment, there are no longer Private Members' motions on Fridays.

As to Private Members' Bills, names are put on ballot papers and a draw takes place at the beginning of each session in the committee room in the presence of the Chairman of Ways and Means. Members who are successful in the ballot and who have no bill of their own may introduce the bill of another Member, or they may present to the House a bill that has already gone through the House of Lords in a previous session. The Government Whips Office also has a number of non-controversial bills that are available for a backbencher who has more luck than imagination. To be fair, these 'off-the-peg' bills have a significantly higher than average chance of success, so this is quite a constructive use of an MP's luck.

A private member cannot promote a bill that would directly involve Government expenditure or taxation. Private Members' Bills pass through the same stages as all public bills. At the report stage, however, any Member can propose amendments, even those rejected in committee. It is the Speaker who decides which amendments should be debated.

A Private Member's Bill faces many difficulties during the legislative process. The Member does not possess the advantage of having parliamentary counsel, and only receives £200 from the Government to help with expenses in drafting the bill. If the bill is uncontroversial, the Member may not find it easy to persuade forty Members to stay at Westminster on a Friday to maintain the necessary quorum. If it is controversial, its opponents will employ all the relevant procedural devices to obstruct the bill. Despite the Jopling changes, its opponents may still try to 'talk it out' at second reading, by filibustering either the bill itself or the bill being debated before it in the House. So if you hear your MP speak at enormous length on a Friday morning about a subject that you never knew he or she was interested in, and you want to know what is going on, look at what is next in the queue. The odds are it's the next bill that he or she is trying to stop.

If an opponent of a bill is speaking just before 2.30 p.m. on a Friday, then one of its advocates must move 'that the question be now put'. Under this Closure procedure, if the Chair agrees to move the Closure, then at least 100 members must vote in favour of the Closure. Getting 100 supporters to attend a Friday debate can be very difficult. This problem can also recur at the report stage.

This need for 100 members in the 'aye' lobby can lead to moments of cliff-hanging suspense. One of the better examples of this occurred in April 1989, when a Private Member's Bill guaranteeing the public the right to reply to a newspaper reporting about them came before the House. It was highly controversial, and exactly 100 MPs went through the 'aye' lobby to vote for closure. One of them, however, negatived his vote by going through the 'no' lobby as well. Norman Tebbit promptly put a point of order, suggesting that the required 100 votes had not been met because one had been negatived. His point of order was put during a division, so he had to make it seated, wearing a top hat. He cut a truly Dickensian figure, looking like nothing so much as a Victorian undertaker, and provoking cries of 'Gradgrind' from the Opposition. He was overruled on his point of order, but his party (against the bill) won the day, and it was talked out.

With all of these procedural gambits available to the opponents of a bill, it is not surprising that almost no controversial Private Members' Bills succeed. The failure of abortion law reform is a good example. Such reform has majority support in the House, even though several attempts to change it have been thwarted. Dennis Skinner even used a by-election writ to talk out the attempt by Ann Widdecombe to reform this law (see Chapter 3). Several years ago John Corrie used up nearly half of all the time for Private Members' Bills that year and his bill on abortion was still thwarted. It was noticeable that when he next drew a high number on the Private Members' ballot, he chose to propose a bill on Fish Diseases, which was successful precisely because it was uncontroversial.

At the committee stage bills can be delayed, as all Private Members' Bills are considered in Standing Committee C. Filibustering one bill can lead to delays to the next waiting in queue for consideration.

UNBALLOTED BILLS

Apart from the ballot, there are two other methods by which Private Members' Bills can be introduced. Standing Order No. 58 (SO No. 58) allows every Member to present a bill of his or her choice. It is fairly rare for this sort of bill to be successful, although the Protection of Birds (Amendment) Bill 1976 passed through all its Commons' stages in sixty-seven seconds.

For SO No. 58 bills to be successful they must be entirely non-controversial, because they are not given a second reading if even one Member objects. Like Ten Minute Rule Bills, SO No. 58s are principally a technique for giving publicity to an idea, rather than a way of creating new laws.

TEN MINUTE RULE BILLS

The second method by which Private Members' Bills may be introduced is under Standing Order No. 19 (SO No. 19) – the so-called Ten Minute Rule Bills. These are not usually expected by their sponsors to become law, but they are a valuable method of allowing back-benchers to express a view on a subject that they feel is important. Normally the intention is to air a controversial subject in prime time. A well-publicized Ten Minute Rule Bill will get coverage on television, Radio 4 and in most quality newspapers. It may signal the opening shot in a campaign.

Ten Minute Rule Bills can be introduced on Tuesday or Wednesday from (usually) the seventh week of each session, just after Question Time. Members have to give notice three weeks in advance that they will be introducing an SO No. 19 Bill. The Member is then allowed to make a ten-minute speech, and only one MP is allowed to speak in opposition, also for ten minutes. After this the Speaker puts the question and, if it is not defeated, it proceeds through the remaining stages as with other legislation.

In 1969–70, Robin Maxwell-Hyslop managed to get seventy Ten Minute Rule slots by handing in the titles at the beginning of the session. To get a Ten Minute Rule Bill slot, an MP had to queue – generally overnight. Now the rules on Ten Minute Rule Bill slots have changed by informal agreement and queuing overnight has virtually ceased, as deals are done between the Government Whips Office and the Opposition Whips Office to allocate them on an alternating basis.

PRIVATE BILLS

Apart from Private Members' Bills, the other principal form of private legislation is the private bill. Private bills are so called because they affect the interests of small and specific groups of individuals or a corporate body. There are sometimes private bills that relate to personal matters, such as marriage, estates and naturalization, although these are now very rare. Most private bills are promoted by companies or local authorities. The Birmingham City Council Act 1985, for example, provides for motor racing to be held on public roads in the city.

Private bills begin when the organization or individual presents a petition to Parliament. Petitions for private bills are inspected by one or other of the examiners on behalf of both Houses, to ensure that they comply with the elaborate standing orders for private business. These require that all people who would be particularly affected by the bill are informed of its provisions.

Petitions may be presented objecting to the proposed private bill, and these are considered in the House of Commons by the Court of Referees to determine whether they can be heard (only if the petitioners have no *locus standi* – if they are directly affected by the bill, for example – which would entitle them to be heard). The bill may then have its first reading and go on to the second reading stage.

Private bills can often be very controversial. For example, in 1989, the bill to allow Associated British Ports to expand their port at Immingham (the ABP [No. 2] Bill) was opposed by MPs representing mining constituencies, who feared that the port would be used to bring in cheap coal and put British miners out of jobs. They therefore tried to oppose and filibuster the bill. In so doing they were supported by the two mining trade unions (the NUM and the UDM) and a coalition of local authorities covering mining areas. The vast majority of the bill's opponents were Labour Members, but there were also some Conservatives representing Nottinghamshire pit areas who opposed the bill.

The second reading was the first opportunity to defeat or delay the bill. Since it was essentially a free-enterprise measure, and added to Britain's port capacity, Conservative (but not Government) support for the bill was reasonably assured. Outright defeat of the bill was therefore highly improbable, so the main weapon of the opponents was delay. This is achieved by tactics designed to convince the Chairman of the Ways and Means Committee (who has the duty of supervising all private legislation; however, any of the Deputy Speakers could preside over a second reading in the House) that not enough time has been given for debate when the time for the vote comes at 10 p.m. If he is so convinced he may then refuse a closure, and the bill is put off for further debate on another day. This delay can be very damaging for a number of reasons. First, time has to be found in the parliamentary timetable and this is always scarce – effectively the Government has to agree to make time for it. Secondly, if the bill has to be carried over into a new session, it is the subject of a 'Carry-over Motion', as a result of which it may be delayed or defeated. Private bills do not queue for committee 'slots' in the same way as Private Members' Bills. More than one Opposed Bill Committee can sit at any time. Committee dates are normally chosen by agreement between the promoters and the petitioners and usually depend on the availability of counsel.

It is worth noting at this point that the power of the Chairman of the Ways and Means Committee is very great. Within the limits of reasonableness – which are quite wide – he has absolute power over whether a closure will be granted. The chairman of Ways and Means at the time of the ABP (No. 2) Bill was Harold Walker, the Member for Doncaster Central – a mining constituency! This undoubtedly tested his impartiality greatly and became the source of controversy at third reading.

If there are no petitions against it, a private bill is referred to the Committee on Unopposed Bills, which questions the bill's promoter to find out if the bill is really necessary. If, like the ABP (No. 2) Bill, it has been opposed in petition, it is sent to the Committee on Opposed Bills, which comprises four MPs, all of whom have to sign a declaration that neither they nor their constituents have any vested interests in the bill. When all evidence for and against the bill has been heard, the committee deliberates in private, and then the chairman reports the committee's recommendations to the House.

Tactics in committee are aimed at getting the bill through unamended. If this is achieved, no amendments on the floor of the House are allowed and the bill goes straight to third reading without a report stage. This dramatically reduces scope for delaying tactics and sharply increases the chances of the bill's becoming law. Because report stage involves debating a series of amendments which can each be put to a vote at any time between 7 p.m. and 10 p.m., it involves Members being on call sometimes for several days. This is what is meant by a 'running Whip', and it is very hard indeed to manage it for a private bill. Thus a report stage creates opportunities for opponents to succeed with all sorts of crippling amendments. Avoidance of report stage is therefore important to achieve if at all possible.

The ABP (No. 2) Bill did achieve this. It was well drafted and was not amended at all in committee. A third reading debate set down for 7 p.m. could be expected to last until 10 p.m. It therefore went straight to third reading, on 25 May 1989. In theory, third reading debates are formal reviews of the principles of a bill and should be short. Nevertheless, the opponents fought a last-ditch campaign. Points of order delayed the start of the substantive debate, but Michael Brown managed to start proceedings at 7.29 p.m. by moving that the bill should be given a third reading. But when he proposed the closure at 9.57 p.m. he was refused. There was terrible confusion. Third readings can go through in one and a half hours. The atmosphere was acrimonious. During the debate there had been allegations that the committee chairman had not been impartial – a very serious accusation. On the other side the sponsor of the bill was furious.

Other than the question of amendment in committee, private bills generally receive their report stage and their third reading in just the same way as Government bills. While Government bills and Private Members' Bills have to complete the whole legislative process through both Houses in a single session, private bills can be suspended and taken up again in the following session.

8

OUT OF THE CHAMBER

The size of the House of Commons' workload prevents it from conducting much of its business within the chamber. Therefore a system has developed whereby business is done by various committees.

SELECT COMMITTEES

Select committees are of two types: departmental and non-departmental.

DEPARTMENTAL SELECT COMMITTEES

The purpose of departmental select committees is 'to examine the expenditure, administration and policy of the principal Government Departments . . . and associated public bodies'. Their permanent establishment was one result of the Conservative victory in the 1979 general election. Prior to that, the system of departmental select committees had been rather incomplete and *ad hoc*. There are now seventeen departmental select committees: Agriculture; Defence; Deregulation; Education and Employment; Environment; Foreign Affairs; Health; Home Affairs; National Heritage; Northern Ireland Affairs; Science and Technology; Scottish Affairs; Social Security; Trade and Industry; Transport; Treasury and Civil Service; and Welsh Affairs. Their work is co-ordinated and supervised by the Liaison Committee, which consists of the chairmen of the committees.

The total membership of these select committees is roughly in proportion to the size of the parties in the Commons. The members of each Committee are chosen by the Committee of Selection and the convention is that Government ministers, parliamentary private secretaries and Opposition front-bench spokesmen and women are not nominated to serve. The chairman of each committee is chosen by the members of that committee.

These committees are able to 'send for persons, papers and records' that are necessary for their inquiry and they then issue reports giving

their opinion and observation upon any matters referred to them for their consideration, together with the minutes of the evidence taken before them, and also to make a special report of any matters which they may think fit to bring to the notice of the House.

While the select committees can make recommendations to the House as to what actions they feel are necessary or desirable, these suggestions will not necessarily be acted upon.

Select committees are, however, able to appoint specialist or technical advisers to assist them and they can insist upon the attendance of any British citizen apart from MPs and peers. Conventionally, Members of the Houses of Parliament do not refuse to give evidence to a select committee. However, this has not always been the case. Edwina Currie refused to appear before the Agriculture Committee on salmonella, and Margaret Beckett declined to give evidence to the Procedure Committee on deregulation orders on the ground that the legislation had not yet been enacted. The committees on Home Affairs, Foreign Affairs and the Treasury and Civil Service are each empowered to appoint one sub-committee. The select committees' power to demand papers and records does not apply to papers and records that are held by Government departments. However, in 1986 the Defence Committee, during its examination of the Westland affair, was given two documents by an unwilling Government. A select committee can ask people or organizations to submit written evidence before they appear before the committee, to give oral evidence and to be questioned. Although most select committee sessions are open to the press and public, they can be held in private if security matters or confidential affairs are to be discussed.

Committee members may also wish to travel somewhere to gather evidence. Often this may simply mean a visit to a defence establishment or a nuclear power station in Britain, but sometimes it is necessary to go abroad.

NON-DEPARTMENTAL SELECT COMMITTEES

There are also the non-departmental select committees. The oldest of these is the Committee of Privileges, which has met, although not continuously, since the seventeenth century. Composed of seventeen of the most experienced and eminent Members of the House, it meets whenever there is a complaint about an alleged breach of parliamentary privilege.

The Public Accounts Committee was established by William Gladstone in 1861. It examines the reports submitted by the Comptroller and Auditor General, who oversees the accounts of each Government department to ensure that the money allocated was spent in the way that Parliament intended, and also to check that the departments have not been wasteful or careless with this money. The Public Accounts Committee is made up of fifteen Members, all of whom are extremely knowledgeable in financial affairs, and is chaired by a senior Opposition MP. It is one of the most respected of all parliamentary committees, because of the expertise of its members and because it is generally non-partisan in a party political sense. The committee can summon the Accounting Officer of each department (usually the Permanent Secretary, the most senior civil servant in the department) to explain his or her department's expenditure, and its findings and recommendations are reported to Parliament and are always taken very seriously by the Treasury.

The Select Committee on European Legislation was set up in 1974 and examines all changes proposed by the European Community. It then decides which of these proposals are sufficiently important, either legally or politically, to be brought to the attention of the whole House. The House of Lords Select Committee on European Legislation is generally considered to have been more effective than the House of Commons at scrutinizing European legislation, which, until recently, had tended to be discussed in the Commons late at night, with the result that only Euro-fanatics attended. However, the Government has been changing this, and attempting to find other ways of making the Commons more effective in terms of examining European legislation.

The Services Committee has been broken into four domestic committees (administration; catering; accommodation and works; and information) which regulate all aspects of accommodation, catering, broadcasting and administration of the House. The Procedures Committee considers whether particular changes to the procedures of the House would be desirable. Occasionally, although now less frequently, *ad hoc* select committees are set up to examine a particular issue. For example, such *ad hoc* select committees investigated obscene publications in 1957, abortion in 1974–5 and MPs' pay in 1980–81 and 1981–2.

The Select Committee on Statutory Instruments, sometimes known as the Scrutiny Committee, was established in 1944 in order to scrutinize all secondary, or delegated, legislation that has been presented to the House and to decide whether the statutory instruments were drafted correctly and clearly and whether all the constitutional and legal procedures that govern the making of legislation have been followed. In reality, this committee scrutinizes relatively few instruments; the bulk of the work is done by the Joint Committee. If the statutory instruments being examined have already been laid before both Houses of Parliament, then the Commons Select Committee and the Lords Select Committee meet jointly.

COMMITTEE OF THE WHOLE HOUSE

Almost every bill used to be considered by a committee of the whole House, which comprises all MPs. Although this committee meets in the chamber of the House itself, it is chaired not by the Speaker but rather by the Chairman of Ways and Means. This convention originated from the period when the Speaker was considered by many to be the king's spy in the House. When the committee is in session, the mace is placed below the table rather than upon it.

Only three types of bill are now considered by a committee of the whole House. First, there are those that are so uncontroversial that their committee stage will last only a few minutes. Secondly, those bills that are so urgent that the legislative process has to be speeded up are dealt with by such a committee. Thirdly, a committee of the whole House examines bills of the utmost constitutional importance, such as a bill to reform the House of Lords, to enter the European Economic Community or to grant devolution to Wales or Scotland. The advantage of considering important and controversial bills by a committee of the whole House is that it allows many more Members than could sit on a standing committee to speak on them. Sometimes part of a bill, such as the Family Law Bill 1996, is considered in a standing committee and part in a committee of the whole House. The Finance Bill always has part of its committee stage in a standing committee and part in a committee of the whole House.

STANDING COMMITTEES

Most bills are considered by a standing committee, the first of which was established in 1882, as part of the campaign to defeat attempts by Parnell's Irish Party to obstruct the business of the House. Most standing committees are named by a letter of the alphabet (Standing Committee A, Standing Committee B and so on). Each committee will deal with several pieces of unconnected legislation one after the other, which may well be in entirely different subject areas. Standing Committee C, in theory, deals only with Private Members' Bills, but in practice these can also go into vacant Government standing committees. After a committee has reported to the House on a piece of legislation, its membership is dismissed. The same committee – for example, A – will then be reconstituted with an entirely different membership to consider another bill.

The membership of each committee is chosen by the Committee of Selection. MPs are nominated for a standing committee because they are interested in the subject of the bill that that committee will be discussing. If MPs are called to speak at the second reading of a bill, they will, as a rule, serve on the standing committee of the bill. Standing committees, which should broadly reflect the strength of the parties in the House, can comprise sixteen–fifty members, including the relevant Government minister, Opposition spokesman or woman and a Whip from both the Government and the main Opposition party.

Scottish standing committees, which consider bills relating exclusively to Scotland, must consist of at least sixteen MPs representing Scottish constituencies. The Scottish Grand Committee no longer has non-Scottish Members added to it. Its business now includes oral questions, ministerial statements, second reading debates on Scottish bills, general debates chosen by political parties and half-hour adjournment debates. There is also a Northern Ireland Grand Committee, which consists of all the Members for Northern Ireland constituencies and up to twenty-five others. There is a similar body for Wales, the Welsh Grand Committee, which consists of all the MPs from Welsh constituencies and five other MPs.

PRIVATE BILL COMMITTEES

Private bills are dealt with in the Private Bill Committee, which comprises only the chairman and three Members and broadly follows the procedure of select committees. Opposed private bills are taken to the Opposed Private Bill Committee, while unopposed bills are taken to the Committee on Unopposed Bills; neither of these is a standing committee.

PARTY COMMITTEES

In addition to these formal parliamentary committees, MPs may also sit on party committees. In the case of the Conservative Party, the most famous of these is the 1922 Committee, formally known as the Conservative Private Members' Committee. All Conservative back-benchers are members of the 1922 Committee, which was formed in 1923 by a group of Members first returned in the 1922 general election. The 1922 Committee is extremely influential and the chairman of its executive committee has the right of access to the party leader.

There are, in addition, various groups of like-minded Conservative MPs, such as the One Nation and Blue Chip groups, which debate issues and plan strategies. Dining clubs, consisting of MPs with common interests, also meet regularly for a meal attended by a guest speaker, and a whole series of Conservative back-bench committees – open to all Conservative back-benchers – exists on a great variety of topics.

The Labour Party also has a wide range of committees which its MPs can join. The Parliamentary Labour Party (PLP) includes all Labour MPs. When the party is in Government, a liaison committee of the PLP, composed mainly of back-benchers but with some ministers, is elected to keep the Government in touch with back-bench opinion. When the Party is in Opposition, an executive committee of the PLP is elected. This comprises the party leader and deputy leader, the Chief Whip, the chairman of the PLP, three peers and fifteen other MPs. The members of this committee are principal front-bench spokesmen and women. There are also subject groups, regional groups and groups of ideologically similar Members, such as the Tribune Group and the Campaign Group.

ALL-PARTY GROUPS

A wide variety of all-party groups have formed in Parliament and these are of two types: subject groups and country groups. There are approximately 100 all-party subject groups, covering a wide range of topics from cycling, engineering, development and the motor industry to pensions, refugees and transport. A similar number of all-party country groups combine their expertise on, for example, America, the Russian Federation, Germany, Norway, Malta, Israel or Uganda.

EARLY DAY MOTIONS

MPs can vent their opinions by proposing or signing an Early Day Motion (EDM). Although their sponsors realize that such motions will not be debated, EDMs are, theoretically, motions for debate at an early opportunity.

EDMs may be of a party political nature or be concerned with a local issue, such as the closing of a hospital, or advocate a change in Government policy. The vast majority of EDMs are parliamentary mechanisms to raise public interest in an issue which would not otherwise gain prominence. For the observer of debates these issues therefore seem far more important than they are. A typical EDM was that sponsored by Jacques Arnold, Norman Tebbit, Michael Heseltine, Nicholas Bennett, John Townend and the author as part of the parliamentary campaign in opposition to the National Dock Labour Scheme:

That this House expresses its grave concern at the continuing existence of the National Dock Labour Scheme; deplores its debilitating effects on the economies of the port areas, most of which are in inner city areas; notes that the scheme has presided over a decline in the number of registered dockers from 78,000 in 1974 to less than 9,500 today; notes that Wharton Econometrics Forecasting Associates Group study that 45,000 extra jobs would have been created in the ports but for the scheme; observes the need to clear these restrictive practices well before 1992; and calls on Her Majesty's Government to make the necessary arrangements to abolish the scheme and set our ports free.

Other MPs use EDMs to draw attention to a cause espoused by a particular pressure group or as a method of pursuing campaigns against groups or individuals they believe to be guilty of wrongdoing – EDMs having the advantage of being immune from libel actions under parliamentary privilege. Some EDMs cover less political topics, from sporting victories to congratulations on the birth of Margaret Thatcher's grandchild.

A Member who wishes to put forward an EDM submits it to the Table Office together with the signatures of the MPs whom he or she has already persuaded to sign it. It is then printed in the notice paper. Other Members can add their names to the motion by informing the Table Office that they wish to support it. In recent times, it has become conventional that ministers do not sign EDMs.

Each EDM is given an identification number – the numbers starting again from one at the beginning of each session. When the EDM receives further support, the motion is reprinted in the notice paper with the names of the Members who are now supporting it and the total number of MPs who have signed.

THE HOUSE OF LORDS

STANDING COMMITTEES

The principal difference between the Lords and Commons committees is that Lords committee stages of bills are virtually all taken on the floor of the House. The Lords do not have the Commons standing committees as such.

SELECT COMMITTEES

The Lords do not have departmental select committees, and their select committees resemble the *ad hoc* structure that existed in the Commons before the recent reforms. They have, for example, a Procedure Select Committee and one on Science and Technology.

The Lords do create the odd select committee to look at a particular subject. One such *ad hoc* select committee in the Lords was on Sustainable Development. Another considers the relationship between central and local government. These are, again, symptomatic of the reflective nature of the Lords.

EARLY DAY MOTIONS

The Lords do not have EDMs and generally they do not favour this sort of 'petition'. They do have, on their order paper, motions for 'No Day Named', but these are put down by peers because they believe the subject should be debated on a Wednesday (the day set aside for motions rather than legislation).

9

THE CABINET

The Treasury bench – the front bench above the gangway on the Government side – is occupied by ministers and Government Whips. Normally, during a debate or Question Time, only the relevant departmental ministers will sit on the bench at any one time. This is simply practical, since they all have massive workloads which require them to be in their departments much of the time, and anyway there is not room on the bench for all of them at the same time. Indeed, when a large number wish to be there, they tend to spill over into the parliamentary private secretaries' bench immediately behind.

For the last few decades, each Government has contained at least 100 members in a ranked hierarchy – Prime Minister, senior Cabinet ministers, other Cabinet ministers, ministers of Cabinet rank but who are not in the Cabinet, junior ministers, Whips and parliamentary private secretaries. Of these 100-plus members of the Government, the most important twenty or so are members of the Cabinet, the policy-making body, which is based almost entirely upon convention and was not mentioned in an Act of Parliament until the Ministers of the Crown Act 1937. On occasion the statutory size of the Cabinet has been expanded by people sitting in the Cabinet without holding a ministerial position. For example, in the 1970s Harold Lever was in the Cabinet without being a Cabinet minister, and in the 1990s Jeremy Hanley, the then Conservative Party Chairman, sat in Cabinet without holding ministerial responsibilities.

THE HISTORY OF THE CABINET

The British Cabinet, as we know it today, is the result of a long process of evolution. The Curia Regis, which was a group of trusted counsellors to whom the Norman kings turned for advice, developed, in the thirteenth century, into the Privy Council, which consisted of various royal officials such as the Treasurer, the Chancellor, the Justiciar and the Secretary. However, over the years, the Privy Council simply grew too large to be an effective policy-making and administrative body. Consequently a new, smaller body of particularly trusted advisers emerged – the Cabinet Council.

The early and middle periods of the eighteenth century saw the beginnings of Cabinet government in Britain. Until the early eighteenth century the king had presided over ministerial Cabinet meetings in person. He accordingly had an enormous personal influence on the formation of policy. In 1714, however, George I ascended the throne. He did not bother to attend Cabinet, at least from 1717 onwards. This created scope in the long term both for a Cabinet that was independent of the Crown and for the development of a Cabinet leader – the Prime Minister.

It was this period that saw the gradual decline in the monarch's political importance. Although the monarch may, in theory, refuse to give assent to any bill, the last time when this power was used was, as already noted, in 1707. The monarch's power to influence political events rested primarily upon his or her ability to ensure that preferred candidates were elected to Parliament (which was achieved through extensive bribery) and secondarily upon his control of MPs (through use of patronage). Sir Robert Walpole, who is generally acknowledged as the first Prime Minister of Britain, even though he never officially took this title, was appointed First Lord of the Treasury in 1721 and held the post until 1742.

Walpole owed much of his tremendous power to the fact that he controlled the Treasury's purses and was thus able to manipulate both elections and, so, the elected MPs. What marked Walpole out from all previous First Lords of the Treasury was that he was able to act as the direct connection between the monarch, the Cabinet and Parliament.

THE ROLE OF THE CABINET

The Cabinet is basically the committee of Members of both Houses of Parliament* which co-ordinates the work of the entire Government.

The Cabinet's role, therefore, is to determine what the Government's policies will be. When it has come to a decision on any aspect of policy, the relevant department will act on this decision if it has the legal powers to do so. If it does not, it will submit a bill to Parliament to have the law changed as necessary.

In theory the Cabinet takes an overview, concerning itself with general policy and not intervening in detail. The extent to which this is the reality depends in part on the personality of the Prime Minister and other Cabinet colleagues and in part on the issues. Sir Winston Churchill's peacetime administration (1951–5) – full of very able Cabinet ministers – was characterized by global vision. By contrast, Harold Wilson's first administration (1964–6) – run by an energetic polymath, with rather inexperienced ministers, following a very interventionist policy – was probably characterized by a more detailed style of Prime Ministerial involvement.

Each minister is expected to make a decision about all relatively unimportant or uncontroversial matters that come before him or her. He or she should refer matters to the Cabinet only if they are of the utmost political importance or if he or she is unable to resolve any difficulties on the issue with the other ministers or departments involved. Inter-departmental issues create great scope for disagreement and dispute, and are accordingly frequently referred to Cabinet. Examples of this include Westland (involving the Department of Trade and Industry and the Ministry of Defence) and the controversy sur-

---

* The only minister who was never an MP or peer was Jan Smuts, the South African leader, who was a member of Lloyd George's War Cabinet.

rounding food and hygiene controls that resulted in Edwina Currie's resignation as a Parliamentary Under-Secretary of State for Health (involving the Ministry of Agriculture, Fisheries and Food and the Department of Health).

SECRECY

The full Cabinet normally meets for two or three hours once or, perhaps, twice each week. Cabinet discussions are supposed to be strictly confidential. All Cabinet members are bound by the Official Secrets Act (which forbids the publication of various official documents), the Privy Councillor's Oath (not to disclose information) and by the convention that it is necessary to have the monarch's permission to reveal Cabinet proceedings because Cabinet decisions are advice to the monarch. This secrecy is important so that Cabinet members may talk freely and frankly in Cabinet, away from the gaze of public scrutiny. However, it is sometimes undermined by the memoirs of former members of the Cabinet and unattributable briefings given by ministers to journalists on an anonymous basis, as well as by 'leaks' from civil servants.

Often this secrecy is for very good reasons. Decisions taken in Cabinet can materially influence commercial concerns – are 'price-sensitive information', in stock-market parlance. Early disclosure would inevitably be to someone's advantage and to someone else's disadvantage. Other areas – for example, where military secrets are involved or perhaps negotiations with other countries or international bodies such as the European Union – must also be kept secret. The fact that the Cabinet has historically been one of the most secretive areas of British Government makes it difficult to make any very detailed analysis of it. As Walter Bagehot wrote in *The English Constitution*, 'The most curious point about the Cabinet is that so very little is known about it.'

THE PRIME MINISTER

The Prime Minister is traditionally spoken of as being only 'first among equals' (*primus inter pares*) among Cabinet members but in reality he or she is ultimately the most powerful individual in the Cabinet, in the Government and in his or her party. Some believe that the power of the Prime Minister is almost unrestrained, but this is very superficial and simplistic. The general argument that there is in Britain a 'presidential' Prime Ministership is based on the following powers. It is the Prime Minister who decides who should become ministers and in what positions. The Prime Minister settles what is to be on the agenda for Cabinet meetings and chairs these meetings. The Prime Minister usually has a large enough majority in the House of Commons to ensure that the Government's legislation is successful. The Prime Minister dominates and personifies his or her party and can rely upon most party members to be loyal supporters of the Government and therefore of him or her. The Prime Minister can threaten to ask the monarch to dissolve Parliament and thus call a general election.

On the other hand, there are many constraints upon their powers. Prime Ministers cannot simply pick whoever they want to be in the Cabinet or Government; they must be guided by the need to include representatives of most ideological and regional groups within the parliamentary party. Prime Ministers may indeed include critics from their own party so that they will be constrained to some extent by the doctrine of collective responsibility. They do not have a free hand with Cabinet discussions and decisions. There are numerous examples, even from the last thirty years, of Prime Ministers being overruled by Cabinet. Senior civil servants are also often able to ensure that the Government's policies do not threaten or challenge the vested departmental interests that undoubtedly exist.

The threat of calling a general election is not a very effective one, since most MPs have 'safe' seats. There is also a limit to the extent to which one man or woman can effectively control the entire Government machine. Finally, the Prime Minister can remain in that office only for as long as he or she has the support of most colleagues in Government and in the parliamentary party.

Sir Robert Walpole holds the record for the longest tenure as Prime Minister, at twenty years and 315 days, from 3 April 1721 to 11 February 1742. Since the reduction in length of terms from seven to five years under the Parliament Act of 1911, only one Prime Minister has been returned to power in three successive general elections, and she is Margaret Thatcher, who also holds the record for the longest-serving PM this century (eleven years and 203 days) and the first woman to hold the position.

DEPUTY PRIME MINISTERS

The role of Deputy Prime Minister dates from 1942, when Winston Churchill appointed Clement Attlee to the post. There was then a clear need for such a post. Committed as Churchill was to pursuing the Second World War, it was useful to have somebody who could worry about more domestic matters. It also helped bond the Labour Party into a coalition Government.

The job disappeared at the end of the war and did not reappear after the 1945 general election. Nor did it come back into existence with the return of Churchill as Prime Minister in 1951, apparently because King George VI did not wish the proposed deputy, Anthony Eden, to become the presumptive heir-apparent.

The post only reappeared officially in 1962, when R. A. Butler was appointed Deputy Prime Minister, with the new title of First Secretary of State. It lapsed again when Sir Alec Douglas-Home became Prime Minister but was reinstated by Harold Wilson in 1964. It disappeared under Edward Heath, returned under Jim Callaghan and was continued under Margaret Thatcher. After Lord Whitelaw retired from the Cabinet in 1988, Sir Geoffrey Howe served as Lord President and Deputy Prime Minister from July 1989 until November 1990, when he stepped down and dramatically turned on his Prime Minister. The post then dropped out of fashion until John Major appointed Michael

Heseltine as First Secretary of State and Deputy Prime Minister in July 1995.

The post has no constitutional existence and is frankly a reflection of the politics and personal chemistry of the Prime Minister and the second-ranking Cabinet minister. Politics matters in that such an appointment might be seen as favouring one candidate for the succession over another. This apparent pre-empting of both the party

---

One Prime Minister's Deputy

Nobody becomes a Prime Minister without having a strong character, and quite frequently he or she needs a deputy who can smooth things over. For Mrs Thatcher for a long time this role was filled by Willie Whitelaw. Some of his sayings, and some sayings about him, give a flavour of what sort of man he was.

Norman Tebbit (in his autobiography): 'Willie was always emollient – when he was getting his own way.'

Willie: 'I don't blame anyone, except, perhaps, all of us.'

'The Archbishop of Canterbury is a very religious man.'

'I have always thought it a great mistake ever to prejudge the past.'

'They are going around the country stirring up complacency.'

'We are examining alternative anomalies.'

'I can assure you that I definitely might take action.'

On Roy Hattersley's appointment as Shadow Home Secretary: 'I could take a man who was straight left. I could stand someone who was straight right. But Hattersley is neither left, right nor straight.'

While Whitelaw was defending a Government decision during a debate, a Labour MP shouted out that Mr Whitelaw had voted against it last time. Mr Whitelaw responded: 'That does not alter the logic of my position.'

Margaret Thatcher: 'Every Prime Minister needs a Willie.'

---

leadership election procedures and the royal prerogative would seem to be the reason behind George VI's vetoing of Anthony Eden and Harold Macmillan's hesitation over R. A. Butler. Mrs Thatcher was more easily able to appoint Willie Whitelaw because he had come second in the leadership contest that she had won but was unlikely to be in the next leadership battle.

Personal chemistry can have varying effects. In the case of Mrs Thatcher and Willie Whitelaw, he was the perfect lieutenant. He was tough but emollient, shrewd but loyal, determined but tactically canny – the perfect foil for a radical, driving, task-orientated Prime Minister. Having, or not having, a Deputy Prime Minister is simply a matter of what works best for that particular Prime Minister.

THE SIZE AND MEMBERSHIP OF THE CABINET

Although the Prime Minister decides on the size and membership of the Cabinet, it is generally wise to include some senior party members because of their political stature, and certain departments have to be represented. Since the end of the Second World War, the size of the Cabinet has been between sixteen and twenty-four members.

In times of great national stress this can contract. When Lloyd George became Prime Minister during the First World War, for example, he formed a War Cabinet of originally only five ministers. The highest membership of this Cabinet was nine. The most interesting point about the War Cabinet was the emphasis placed on members not having any departmental responsibilities. Only two of the nine members were also running Government departments – Bonar Law (the Chancellor) and Neville Chamberlain (the Director-General of National Service). Even the Foreign Secretary, Lord Balfour, was not an official member of the War Cabinet, although he did attend all its meetings. After the successful conclusion of the war, the War Cabinet was disbanded and a Cabinet of more traditional size was formed. The Second World War also caused a small Cabinet to be formed. Neville Chamberlain's War Cabinet consisted of nine members and when

Churchill took over as Prime Minister in May 1940, this number went down to five, although he later increased it to eight. Again, when the war was over, the Cabinet resumed its more normal size.

The Cabinet
(in August 1996)

Prime Minister, First Lord of the Treasury and Minister for the Civil Service
The Rt Hon. John Major, MP

First Secretary of State and Deputy Prime Minister
The Rt Hon. Michael Heseltine, MP

Lord Chancellor
The Rt Hon. The Lord Mackay of Clashfern

Chancellor of the Exchequer
The Rt Hon. Kenneth Clarke, QC, MP

Secretary of State for the Home Department
The Rt Hon. Michael Howard, QC, MP

Secretary of State for Foreign and Commonwealth Affairs
The Rt Hon. Malcolm Rifkind, QC, MP

President of the Board of Trade (Secretary of State for Trade and Industry)
The Rt Hon. Ian Lang, MP

Lord President of the Council and Leader of the House of Commons
The Rt Hon. Tony Newton, OBE, MP

Secretary of State for the Environment
The Rt Hon. John Gummer, MP

Secretary of State for Social Security
The Rt Hon. Peter Lilley, MP

Chief Secretary to the Treasury
The Rt Hon. William Waldegrave, MP

Secretary of State for Northern Ireland
The Rt Hon. Sir Patrick Mayhew, QC, MP

Secretary of State for National Heritage
The Rt Hon. Virginia Bottomley, MP

Secretary of State for Education and Employment
The Rt Hon. Gillian Shephard, MP

Secretary of State for Defence
The Rt Hon. Michael Portillo, MP

Minister without portfolio
The Rt Hon. Dr Brian Mawhinney, MP

Secretary of State for Health
The Rt Hon. Stephen Dorrell, MP

Lord Privy Seal and Leader of the House of Lords
The Rt Hon. The Lord Cecil of Essenden

Secretary of State for Transport
The Rt Hon. Sir George Young, MP

Minister of Agriculture, Fisheries and Food
The Rt Hon. Douglas Hogg, QC, MP

Secretary of State for Scotland
The Rt Hon. Michael Forsyth, MP

Chancellor of the Duchy of Lancaster
The Rt Hon. Roger Freeman, MP

Secretary of State for Wales
The Rt Hon. William Hague, MP

Some people have argued that a 'super Cabinet' should be created, composed of around only six members who should, possibly, have no departmental duties. The purpose of such a super Cabinet would be to formulate broad policy, while the administration of policy would be left to departmental committees. It is argued that a small Cabinet would be able to concentrate on long-term policy formulation and evaluation and would be able to curb any Prime Minister who tried to become too powerful. Against this, however, is the argument that it is not easy to compartmentalize policy-making and administrative functions and a Cabinet composed of only the most senior party figures could easily become too remote from the rest of the Government and from Parliament. It is also hard to see how such figures would be accountable to Parliament in the normal way.

It is, however, true that most Governments already have a form of 'inner Cabinet'. The majority of all Government business falls under the broad headings of home affairs, economic affairs, foreign affairs and defence and, consequently, the ministers who are primarily responsible for these categories will tend to have a very much greater influence on Government policy. These inner groups tend to meet informally on an *ad hoc* basis but in 1969 Harold Wilson established a 'Parliamentary Committee' of six senior Cabinet members under his chairmanship and this development was seen by many as denoting the formal establishing of an inner Cabinet.

COLLECTIVE RESPONSIBILITY

'It doesn't matter what we say, as long as we all say the same thing.' *Lord Melbourne*

One of the most important conventions regarding the Cabinet system is that of collective responsibility. Collective responsibility means that all ministers are bound to support in public all Government policies and Cabinet decisions. If they feel unable to do so, they are required to resign. This also means that the whole Government must resign if it is defeated in the House of Commons on a vote of No Confidence.

The convention of collective responsibility was explained by Joseph Chamberlain as absolute frankness in our private relations and full discussion of all matters of common interest ... the decisions freely arrived at should be loyally supported and considered as the decisions of the whole of the Government. Of course there may be occasions in which the difference is of so vital a character that it is impossible for the minority ... to continue their support and in this case the ministry breaks up or the minority member or members resign.

The rule applies not just to Cabinet members but also to junior ministers and now to the (unpaid) parliamentary private secretaries as well, even though the last are strictly speaking not members of the Government. (In 1967, seven parliamentary private secretaries were dismissed for abstaining on a vote of entry to the EEC.)

The rule has been suspended three times in order to allow ministers to disagree publicly without having to resign. The first occasion was in 1932, when the coalition National Government's 'agreement to differ' applied to the question of tariff protection. In 1975 Labour ministers were allowed to speak publicly against the Government's policy which favoured staying in the European Community. However, Eric Heffer was asked to resign as Minister of State for Industry for criticizing this policy in the House of Commons. The third occasion was in 1977, when Labour ministers were also allowed to disagree publicly on the issue of which electoral system should be used for elections to the European Parliament.

Over the years many ministers have resigned because they could not support an aspect of the Government's policy: for example, Frank Cousins in 1966 and George Brown in 1968. Ian Gow resigned in 1985 because he disagreed with the Government's policy on Northern Ireland, and both Nigel Lawson and Sir Geoffrey Howe resigned, in 1989 and 1990 respectively, because of differences with Mrs Thatcher over Europe. There are, however, examples of ministers criticizing the Government publicly without being asked to resign. In 1969, the then Home Secretary, Jim Callaghan, publicly opposed the Labour Government over trade union reforms. Eventually the Government withdrew its proposed reforms in the face of mounting pressure. Again, in 1974, three Labour ministers criticized the Government's relationship with South Africa but were not dismissed.

When Michael Heseltine resigned in January 1986 as Secretary of State for Defence, he gave his reason as dissatisfaction with the Prime Minister's use of the Cabinet system during the Westland issue. At the press conference at which he announced his resignation, Michael Heseltine commented that Mrs Thatcher's management of the Cabinet system was 'not a proper way to carry on government and ultimately not an approach for which I can share responsibility'.*

The main argument used by critics of Mrs Thatcher's style of leadership was that she simply ignored the Cabinet system, preferring to conduct much business by asking a Cabinet colleague to write a paper on a specific topic for her alone and then summoning that person to come and answer questions on his or her paper. These meetings also included top officials and political advisers. A great deal of policy decisions were reached in this way and this practice was cited as further evidence that Mrs Thatcher was a 'presidential' Prime Minister, with no regard for Cabinet government. Nevertheless, a large part of the success of the Cabinet system has lain in the ability of ministers to reach an agreed conclusion by informal discussion.

The practice is not constitutionally improper and, moreover, it is administratively effective for business to be conducted in the way that Mrs Thatcher preferred. Indeed, it is not new or even particularly unusual. Certainly the pre-eminence of a Prime Minister is not unusual. The decision of Cabinet often takes the form of a Prime Ministerial summary of the debate. Winston Churchill was reputed to have frequently given a magisterial 'summary' of Cabinet discussion, which concluded with a decision completely at odds with the actual discussion that had taken place.

It is even debatable whether Mrs Thatcher diminished Cabinet government in the first place. On the one hand, her critics point to factors such as the reduced number of Cabinet papers since 1979 and that Cabinet only met once a week. On the other hand, Peter Hennessy

* From Peter Hennessy, *Cabinet*

(probably the most knowledgeable journalist on the workings of government in Britain), in *Cabinet*, quoted a 'Whitehall insider' as saying, 'Ministers report to Cabinet pretty freely and frankly. She [Mrs Thatcher] has a passion for knowing what is going on and will be extremely cross if she isn't told.'

Some scepticism is in order about Ministers' dissatisfaction with Cabinet discussions. Even Cabinet-rank ministers can be guilty of simply being the pawns of their civil servants, even on non-departmental matters.

The whole system of Cabinet government, then, requires that as little business as possible is brought before the full Cabinet and that as much as possible is settled through ministerial correspondence, informal consultation and Cabinet committees. The role of the full Cabinet is to discuss only those issues that could not be settled in any other way, as well as the most major controversial policies. As we have already seen, this had become the conventional way of conducting Cabinet government long before Mrs Thatcher or John Major became Prime Ministers.

CABINET COMMITTEES

The growing complexity of government and the huge workload of ministers has led to committees of the Cabinet becoming very much more important post-Second World War. Cabinet committees take two forms: standing committees and *ad hoc* committees. Standing committees are used to deal with problems that would otherwise occupy the full Cabinet regularly. The first such committee was the Committee of Imperial Defence, set up in 1902. *Ad hoc* Cabinet committees have an earlier origin – for example, the Reform Bill 1832 was drafted by such a committee. If ministers dissented from the recommendation of a Cabinet committee, they could then take the matter to a meeting of the full Cabinet and seek to have the original decision overturned. However, John Mackintosh wrote in *The Times* (2 June 1968):

The old system whereby any minister who disliked a committee decision could 'reserve his position' and thus take the matter to the full Cabinet has ended. Mr Wilson has given instructions that when the general opinion of the committee is clear and the chairman is satisfied, that is the end of the matter.

Tremendous secrecy traditionally surrounded the title, membership and work of Cabinet committees, as seen in these two written parliamentary questions and answers:

MR MIKE THOMAS: Would the Prime Minister now answer questions on the membership and terms of reference of Cabinet committees.

THE PRIME MINISTER (MRS MARGARET THATCHER): I have established four standing committees of the Cabinet: a Defence and Overseas Policy Committee and an Economic Strategy Committee, both under my chairmanship; a Home and Social Affairs Committee under the chairmanship of my Right Hon. Friend the Home Secretary; and a Legislation Committee under the chairmanship of the Lord Chancellor. Attendance at these committees will vary according to the subject under discussion. Where appropriate, sub-committees of the standing committees will be established. Membership and terms of reference of the standing committees or their sub-committees will remain confidential.

MR AUSTIN MITCHELL: To ask the Prime Minister, pursuant to her answer on 26 October, in what way it would infringe the principle of collective responsibility to give further details of Cabinet committees and sub-committees.

THE PRIME MINISTER: Under the principle of collective responsibility, all members of the Government are jointly responsible for all the Government's policies and decisions. The publication of details of Cabinet committees and sub-committees would tend to imply that ministers shared responsibility only for decisions in committees of which they were members.

The membership and terms of reference of ministerial committees and sub-committees of the Cabinet are now published. The latest list, compiled in May 1992, counts twenty-five ministerial committees, including the Ministerial Committee on Economic and Domestic Policy, Defence and Overseas Policy, Nuclear Defence Policy, Terrorism, Drug Misuse and Women's Issues.

A typical 'term of reference' for a ministerial committee (for example, the Ministerial Committee on Economic and Domestic Policy) reads 'To consider strategic issues relating to the Government's economic and domestic policies.'

Cabinet committees are also heavily influenced by the nature of the principal minister(s) involved. For example, during Mrs Thatcher's Government the fact that the Falklands were not very evident on the agenda of the Cabinet Overseas and Defence Committee during 1982 was a reflection that the Foreign Secretary, Lord Carrington, did not like bringing Foreign Office business to committee in front of his colleagues.

THE CABINET OFFICE

The Cabinet Secretariat, or Cabinet Office as it is more commonly known, was created by Lloyd George in 1916. Before then there was no formal agenda for Cabinet meetings and the decisions taken were not officially recorded in any minutes but simply noted by the Prime Minister. This obviously led to confusion on many occasions. The Prime Minister would send a letter informing the monarch of the Cabinet's decisions. Ministers would forget what decisions had actually been reached and so their private secretaries would have to telephone the Prime Minister's private secretary in order to discover what had been decided.

The head of the Cabinet Office is the Secretary of the Cabinet, who is the highest-ranking civil servant and has, arguably, the most powerful job in the land after the Prime Minister. The best-known recent Cabinet Secretary was Sir Robert Armstrong, who had the thankless task of appearing in the Australian *Spycatcher* trials in 1987.

The Cabinet Office manages policy areas, such as home and social affairs, security and intelligence, that span many departments of state. The diagram overleaf shows exactly how the information flows, both for budget and operations. The Cabinet Office also compiles the agenda and records and circulates the minutes or 'conclusions' of meetings of

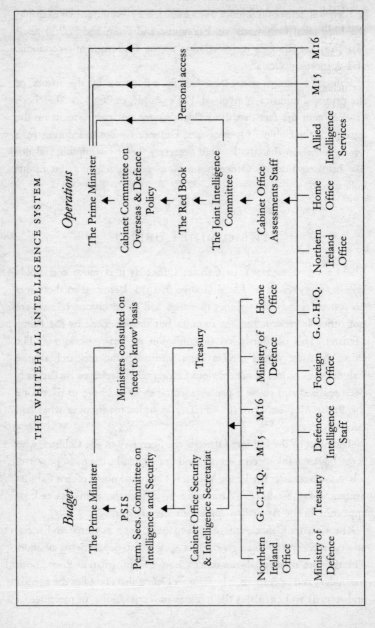

THE WHITEHALL INTELLIGENCE SYSTEM

Operations

The Prime Minister ← Personal access ← M16

M15

Allied Intelligence Services

Cabinet Committee on Overseas & Defence Policy

The Red Book

The Joint Intelligence Committee

Cabinet Office Assessments Staff

Home Office

Northern Ireland Office

Home Office · G.C.H.Q. · Foreign Office · Defence Intelligence Staff · M16 · M15 · G.C.H.Q. · Treasury · Northern Ireland Office

Ministry of Defence

Budget

The Prime Minister

PSIS
Perm. Secs. Committee on Intelligence and Security

Ministers consulted on 'need to know' basis

Treasury

Cabinet Office Security & Intelligence Secretariat

Ministry of Defence · Treasury · Defence Intelligence Staff

the Cabinet and Cabinet committees, and circulates the documents relevant to the agenda to the members of the Cabinet and its committees.

The Cabinet rises and goes to its dinner,
The Secretary stays and gets thinner and thinner,
Scratching his brains to record and report
What he thinks they think that they ought to have thought.

DEPARTMENTS OF STATE

There are a number of departments of state, covering the entire range of Government policies and their administration. Each department has at least one Cabinet minister, occasionally two, as its political head, backed up by a team of more junior ministers. The civil servants in a department are headed by a permanent secretary. The term 'secretary' can cause confusion to outsiders – indeed, on one ministerial trip to China, the title of the permanent secretary who went with the minister was translated into Chinese as 'everlasting typist'. Do not be fooled – the permanent secretaries are some of the most powerful people in Whitehall, the 'Sir Humphreys' of *Yes, Minister* fame. Unlike Sir Humphrey, however, they are generally enormously committed, altruistic and extremely intelligent people.

THE TREASURY

'There are two problems in my life. The political ones are insoluble and the economic ones are incomprehensible.' *Sir Alec Douglas-Home*

'With Sir J. Mennes to Whitehall, where met by W. Batten and Lord Brounker, to attend the King and Duke of York at the cabinet; but nobody had determined what to speak of, but only in general to ask for money.' *Samuel Pepys*

The most important department is the Treasury, which is at the very heart of the whole Government machine. Its main functions are to raise revenue, to regulate public expenditure by the other departments and to oversee the national economy.

The Treasury is represented in Cabinet by the Chancellor of the Exchequer and by the Chief Secretary to the Treasury (although it should not be forgotten that the Prime Minister is First Lord of the Treasury). The importance of the Chancellor's role and the necessary closeness with the Prime Minister are reflected in the fact that the Chancellor's official residence is No. 11 Downing Street. This is next door to the Prime Minister's official residence and indeed has an interconnecting door. Other than the Chancellor of the Exchequer, the Treasury is represented in the Houses of Parliament by the Chief Secretary, the Financial Secretary, the Paymaster General and a minister of state.

The other two great departments of state, the Home Office and the Foreign Office, were created in 1782 out of the old Northern and Southern Departments ('Northern' and 'Southern' referred to their relevant responsibilities within Europe, those within the UK being divided between the two departments on a subject basis). As the sole general department of state concerned with domestic affairs, it was inevitable that the Home Office should become the 'parent' of a succession of other departments, the first of which was the Board of Trade, formed in 1786.

THE FOREIGN OFFICE

'In this dispatch you have used every cliché known to the English language, except "God is love" and "Please adjust your dress before leaving." ' *Winston Churchill*, admonishing the Foreign Office

The Foreign Office, or to give it its full title the Foreign and Commonwealth Office, was in its early days a very aristocratic place. Blue blood was a necessary qualification if one aspired to join the thirty or forty people who made up the Office until the turn of the twentieth century. Today the Foreign Office is much bigger, and its élitism is intellectual. Like the Treasury, it attracts the very brightest civil servants. Unlike the Treasury, the lack of contact with other ministers, and the lack of interchange of staff (most Foreign Office staff being 'lifers'), creates a slightly aloof isolation – perhaps the last hangover of its aristocratic past.

This 'distance' is reflected in the perception of Foreign Office ministers in the Commons. The Office is widely perceived as having favourites – Arabs, Americans and Germans, for example – as well as a less favourable view of others – most particularly the French. Whether or not it is true, this creates an antagonistic reaction among back-benchers who do not agree with these preferences and who often see the Office as representing foreigners in Britain rather than Britain to foreigners.

As a result Foreign Secretaries are known, occasionally, to distance themselves from their department. Lord Carrington is said to have read out his departmental brief at one Cabinet meeting and finished with, 'That, Prime Minister, is what I was told to say and it seems to me to be a load of rubbish.' On another occasion, in the face of parliamentary opposition, he also abandoned an Office initiative (that could possibly have averted the Falklands war). This demonstrates that the democratic process does not always generate the right answers.

Normally the Foreign Office is represented in Parliament by the Foreign Secretary, four ministers of state and a parliamentary under-secretary.

THE HOME OFFICE

The principal functions of the Home Office are maintenance of law and order, with responsibility for prisons, police (indirectly), fire services, civil defence, magistrates' courts, immigration and the Royal Family. As can be seen, its age and generality mean that the Home Office has, over the years, retained a ragbag of responsibilities; many of them are hypersensitive, however, particularly in the field of civil liberties.

The Home Office is represented in the Houses of Parliament by the Home Secretary, three ministers of state and one parliamentary under-secretary.

OTHER DEPARTMENTS

In addition to these three great departments, there exist some 'super ministries'. The Department of the Environment, for example, fills a number of soulless concrete towers in Marsham Street, having been created in 1970 by a merger of the Local Government, Works, Housing and Transport departments, although Transport was subsequently made a department on its own again. It is singularly ironic that this department, responsible for planning, and, until recently, for English Heritage, should be accommodated in what should be a contender for the ugliest government building in London.

The Department of the Environment is responsible for a very wide range of policy, including local government finance, water, the countryside, regional planning, natural disasters, housing and pollution control. This 'super ministry' has a secretary of state, three ministers of state and two parliamentary under-secretaries. Including a Whip, this makes seven people on the ministerial payroll.

The other 'super ministry' with a huge remit is the Department of Trade and Industry, which has one secretary of state (President of the Board of Trade), three ministers of state, three parliamentary under-secretaries and a Whip. These are only some of the largest departments of state. Others include Health, Transport, Social Security, Northern Ireland, Wales, Scotland, Education and Defence.

MINISTERIAL RESPONSIBILITY

'My only great qualification for being put in charge of the Navy is that I am very much at sea.' *Sir Edward Carson*

Ministers have a variety of roles: as well as having departmental responsibilities, they are still Members of Parliament and need to attend party meetings and deal with their constituents' problems. Some ministers employ a political adviser to aid them with their departmental work. Each minister has a departmental Private Office, staffed by civil servants who are normally young and ambitious for rapid promotion. Private Offices supply ministers with the information they need for their ministerial meetings, draft their speeches and letters to MPs, control their ministerial diary and generally take care of all their requirements as Government ministers.

Senior ministers – and occasionally very busy junior ministers – may have a parliamentary private secretary who is a back-bench MP chosen by the minister him- or herself to assist with parliamentary duties. A PPS receives no extra salary for this role and strictly speaking he or she is not a member of the Government. Indeed, some think it is no coincidence that the initials PPS on a letter are used to denote an afterthought. The job of the PPS is to act as a link between the minister and back-bench MPs by keeping in touch with the MPs' opinions on the work and responsibilities of the minister. They also act as a link between ministers and their civil servants when they are in the Palace of Westminster. For example, because civil servants are not allowed on the floor of the chamber, the PPS might be used to pass messages between the civil servants and the minister.

PPSs are not allowed to speak in the House on the work of their minister's department and are expected not to vote against the Government. Such a position is often regarded as being the first step on the road to promotion and ministerial office, although by no means all PPSs do manage to progress further.

The commonest definition of the convention of ministerial responsibility is that ministers are accountable and answerable to Parliament for everything done in their departments, whether committed by themselves or by civil servants of any rank and wherever located.

Under the convention, a minister is expected to appear regularly in Parliament to answer Members' questions about the work of his or her department and matters that fall within its control. Debates upon the policy of a particular department will be opened and closed by ministers from that department. Similarly, when a department is introducing legislation, it is the minister concerned who brings in the bill and defends it during the legislative process.

If responsibility encompasses resignation 'when things go wrong', the convention is not so simple in practice as it is in theory. Obviously, when a minister is personally at fault, he would be expected to resign. John Profumo, for example, resigned in 1963 when it was discovered that he had lied to the House of Commons. In cases where a minister is personally identified with a policy that is not acceptable to either the Government or Parliament, then he or she too would be expected to resign unless the Prime Minister and the Cabinet were prepared to stand behind him or her, in which case the convention of collective responsibility protects that minister. In 1962 the Chancellor, Selwyn Lloyd, was asked to resign because one of his policies was found to be unpopular even though it had previously been supported by the whole Cabinet.

THE MINISTER AS POLICY-MAKER

As the head of a department, it is the minister who formally decides the policy of his or her department. However, now that most departments are such huge decision-making structures, the minister will have little or no knowledge of most of the decisions taken on his or her behalf by the department. Critics of the convention of ministerial responsibility argue that it is meaningless because, in practice, ministers are never held responsible for the actions of their civil servants. This is simply not the case.

The conventions of the British political system are not supposed to be inflexible and precise. Because of the wide variety of situations that could arise under the convention of ministerial responsibility, it is necessary that there can be some degree of discretion and judgement in assessing each particular situation. The practice is that, if an action is carried out on a minister's explicit instructions or is such that the minister can reasonably be expected to have known about it, or if the action was only possible because of inadequate supervision on the part of the minister, then he is expected to resign, as did Sir Thomas Dugdale in 1954. Similarly, the Foreign Secretary, Lord Carrington, and two of his junior ministers resigned after Argentina invaded the Falkland Islands in 1982. A minister cannot be expected to resign because of an action that was carried out against his or her instructions or was of such a level that he or she could not possibly have been expected to know about it. In such cases, however, the minister is still accountable to Parliament and would be expected to explain to the House what had happened and announce measures designed to prevent a recurrence.

Even in the case of action taken by civil servants, it is still the minister who is responsible to Parliament, except in the particular case of the Accounting Officer, whose duty is clearly defined as being separate from that of the minister. Although civil servants may be very important in terms of policy-making, the theory is that they are only able to help ministers to take decisions. Thus the convention of ministerial responsibility is crucially important with respect to the political control exercised by democratically elected ministers over bureaucrats. It ensures a strong political content in the work of a department and prevents any significant delegation of politically sensitive business to bureaucrats and administrators.

11

THE WHIPS OFFICE

The Controller of the Household, the Vice-Chamberlain of the Household and the Lord High Commissioners of the Treasury may sound a little like the cast of a Gilbert and Sullivan opera, but in fact they are the officers of one of the Government's most important arms, the Government Whips Office. It is a department surrounded in mystique. It never issues a press release or a public statement of any kind. Its members never make speeches in the chamber. It and the Opposition Whips Office are only referred to in the chamber by the cryptic phrase the 'usual channels'. The department's name is said to derive from the 'whippers in' – the people who control the hounds at a fox-hunt. This conjures up an image of its operations that further adds to its mystique.

THE ROLE OF THE WHIPS OFFICE

In reality the Whips Office does three jobs. First, and most importantly, it is responsible for managing the Government's business in the House, getting the bills through the House with sufficient votes in reasonable time. Secondly, it is the Government's 'intelligence arm' among its own back-benchers, feeding back to ministers back-bench views on Government policies, and in particular warning them if there are likely to be rebellions. Finally, it is the Government's parliamentary personnel department, monitoring people's performance and recommending individuals for appointment to ministerial office.

Managing the Government's business involves ensuring that Parliament has enacted all the laws that the Government intends by the end of any parliamentary session. Since Parliament is in theory the 'watchdog of the Crown', its rules are designed to protect the individual MP's right to challenge and question the actions of the Government. This inevitably gives some advantage to the Opposition, which can, if it chooses, disrupt the whole proceedings of the House. The Government, in turn, has methods of dealing with this (such as the guillotine), but these inevitably curtail the democratic right of debate (see Chapter 5). Normally it is to the advantage of both sides to co-operate. This co-operation is organized by the Government Whips talking to the Opposition Whips.

The end result is that 'the Government gets its way, but the Opposition gets its say'. Such co-operation is, of course, guarded. Often the Opposition will attempt to 'ambush' the Government. There are many ways to do this, involving use of the complex rules of the House. To do their job properly, both Opposition and Government Whips have to be expert tacticians, well schooled in the mechanics of Parliament and masters of the machine.

The Whips exercise their control of back-bench MPs by issuing, each week, the 'Parliamentary Whip'. This is a document – marked 'Secret' but to be found alongside photocopiers throughout Parliament on many a Friday morning – that outlines the proceedings for the coming week. Each item is underlined. One line means that the business is non-contentious or an issue on which the Government is neutral. Two lines denote that the Government expects opposition, and so most back-benchers (and ministers) are expected to turn up. Three lines mean that everybody is required to turn up to vote unless they have explicit clearance to do otherwise – hence the term 'issuing a Three Line Whip'.

At any one time most back-benchers will support their party and obey the Whip, be it Government or Opposition. There will always be some who oppose it, however. Whatever the reason for disagreement – constituency considerations, ideological reasons, simple differences of judgement – it is at this stage that the Whips' organization swings into action.

THE RESPONSIBILITIES OF THE WHIPS

Each Whip has specific departmental and regional responsibilities. For a controversial piece of legislation, the regional Whips will assess the opinion among their own MPs; the departmental Whip will collate these views.

MPs who disagree with their party's policy to the extent of voting against it are expected to explain their reasons to the Whips. The Whip will first try to convince dissident Members that they should change their mind. If that fails then the Whip will generally organize a meeting between the Member and the minister (or front-bench spokesman or woman) responsible for the policy. The minister will then try to persuade the Member to change his or her mind, sometimes by clarification of the policy, sometimes even by a minor amendment to it.

If Members are still not persuaded, they are next put under considerable pressure. Their local party may criticize them, and that can be quite threatening: Labour MPs have to secure reselection before each general election and thus face deselection, and local Conservative Party associations occasionally open out the selection list even when there is a sitting MP. If they are young, with ambitions of achieving ministerial office, it may be intimated that their careers are at risk – although this is rarely spelled out quite so crudely. What is certain is that the Whips Office will make a judgement as to what will be most effective in persuading dissidents to support their party.

The means of persuasion vary tremendously, as is highlighted by a story once related to me by a minister about his own treatment when he was a back-bencher. He was involved in organizing a rebellion against a Government bill, in alliance with another Conservative MP who shared an office with him. They had both resisted the persuasions of the Whips and the minister, and it was the day before the crucial vote. Peter X and Jack Y (as we shall call them for the purposes of this story) were both working in their office. The phone rang. Jack picked it up. 'Mr Y?' said a curt voice on the phone. 'The Chief wants to see you. In his office. Now.' The phone clicked silent before Jack could respond. With some trepidation, he got to his feet and went down to the Chief Whip's office.

Then minutes later he returned to his own office, white with anger. He related how there had been six Whips waiting in the office, how he had been kept standing while he was berated, shouted at, accused of disloyalty, threatened and finally thrown out without a chance of reply. At that moment the phone rang again. 'Mr X?' asked the curt voice again. 'The Chief wants to see you. In his office. Now.' Peter stood up. He was more than a little nervous as he slowly walked down the stairs to the Chief Whip's office. He knocked on the door.

'Come in,' said a voice. He opened the door. 'Ah, Peter, how nice to see you,' said the Chief Whip pleasantly, standing alone behind his desk. 'Do have a seat. What can I get you to drink? Whisky?' The interview was pleasant and consisted entirely of pointing out how embarrassing for the Government 'this little problem' was and could he possibly reconsider his actions? Different horses for different courses.

That particular Chief Whip is long gone, but it is out of such events that the reputation of the Whips Office is made. More often than not the Whips are pleasant people attempting to do a difficult job with even more difficult people. As one MP said of them recently; 'You have to make allowances. After all, they're just mice trying to be rats.'

While the process of persuasion goes on, the Whips will judge the strength of opposition to the measure being considered. If it is thought that there is a risk of the House not being willing to pass the measure – a possibility of defeat in the chamber – then the policy may be reconsidered. Sometimes the Whips Office misjudges the strength of opposition to a measure: the Home Office proposals in the 1980s for reforming Sunday trading hours, for example, were rejected by the House of Commons. More recently, especially since the Government's majority was reduced, the Whips Office found it almost impossible to control the so-called 'Euro-sceptic' Conservative MPs, and the Whip was briefly withdrawn from the most vociferous of them.

THE CHIEF WHIP

The Chief Whip does not speak in debates. He – there has yet to be a female Chief Whip – is, however, in the chamber more often than many ministers, sitting on the front bench immediately above the gangway. He, or his deputy, can be seen occasionally passing a note to a minister who is speaking at the dispatch box. The note generally says, 'One minute left' and warns the minister that he or she is about to run out of time before the vote. Occasionally the Whip can be seen tugging at the coat-tails of the more garrulous ministers to get them to sit down! Such a scene reflects the permanent concern with time and completion of business that fills the life of the Chief Whip.

Constitutionally taciturn, the nature of the job tends to mean that Chief Whips are tight-lipped and tough-minded. The Chief, as he is known, cuts a very important figure in the House, although he is inevitably something of an *éminence grise*. He is, after all, the man who nominates people to the Prime Minister for most or all of the ministerial posts. It is not for nothing that he is known as Patronage Secretary! Even though he is not technically a member of the Cabinet (although he attends it), his importance is woven into the fabric and traditions of the House. Little things tell all. Tradition has it that he is the only person who has a reserved table in the Members' dining room. Tradition – and practice – in the dining room is that any Member can sit anywhere, even next to the most senior member of the Government. But nobody, not even a Cabinet minister, sits at the Chief's table except by invitation.

There are good reasons for this. The Whips are the only Members of the House who are, in effect, always on duty. They are frequently discussing tactical matters that have to be secret even to their own party. Furthermore, the performance and personality of the ministers and Members are the very stuff of their plans – and obviously not information that is comfortably discussed in an open forum.

The Chief Whip sits as a member of both FLG and LG to help determine exactly what legislation will come before the House. As a pivotal member of these committees, his job can reasonably be described as one of the most powerful in the land, certainly outside of the Cabinet, and probably more so than some within. With this combination of power and insight, it is not surprising that a number of modern Chief Whips have gone on to greater positions, including, in one case, being Prime Minister (Edward Heath).

THE HOUSE OF LORDS

It is difficult to assess party balance accurately in the Lords, because a large number of peers attend only infrequently, the vast majority of whom are Conservative in their affiliations. Moreover, the House of Lords contains the bishops and archbishops and the many other members who express no party affiliations but do not count themselves as 'Crossbenchers'. However, the nominal figures for 1995 of peers who have taken the oath of allegiance are as follows:

Conservative	474
Crossbench	287
Labour	110
Liberal Democrat	52
Others	198

The job of whipping in the House of Lords is therefore very different from that in the Commons. Few peers have any aspirations to Government or party office, so the Whips cannot hold out that as an incentive to follow the party line. There are no sanctions against rebels, and any peer can always get an amendment called. With the 'active' majority being so slender, it is no surprise that the House of Lords frequently amends Government legislation. For big issues, however, the Government Whip (with a Conservative Government) can call up large numbers of 'inactive' peers to vote for a Government measure. This happened with the Community Charge, for example.

The style of whipping in the Lords is also completely different from the Commons. It requires a very light touch, and great skill in the art of persuasion. Sometimes these arts are less orthodox than one might imagine. One Government Chief Whip was renowned for his hospitality, serving the best (and strongest) Bloody Marys in London. He would frequently call a peer in and attempt to dissuade him or her from a particular course of action. He would serve a Bloody Mary while he talked. He would serve another and talk some more. And so it would go on, until, by either persuasion or incapacity, the rebel collapsed – or at least the argument did!

If whipping in the Commons is management by bloody-mindedness, whipping in the House of Lords is management by Bloody Mary.

12

THE ANATOMY OF TWO CAMPAIGNS

What makes a campaign for a change in the law successful? Is it general popularity of the measure? Is it media support? Is it timing? Is it risk or, rather, lack of it? Or does it simply come down to Lord Hailsham's adage, 'The best way I know to win an argument is to start by being in the right.'

To assess this, we can look at two highly controversial campaigns, one of which ended in failure, despite being very popular, and the other of which ended in success, despite being very risky. The first of these campaigns was the attempt to relax the limits on Sunday trading – the Shops Bill – which failed (restrictions on Sunday trading were finally relaxed, although not removed altogether, by the Sunday Trading Act 1994). The second was the abolition of the Dock Labour Scheme – the Dock Work Bill – which received Royal Assent in July 1989. The sequence of events that led, respectively, to failure and to success is shown in the panels which follow.

Shops Bill 1986

1956–82

There were nineteen separate Government Bills, Private Members' Bills and Ten Minute Rule Bills, all designed to change the existing shops legislation. Of these, only two were successful – the Shops (Airports) Act 1962 and the Shops (Early Closing Days) Act 1965.

February 1983

Private Member's Bill introduced by Ray Whitney to remove

---

limitations on Sunday trading fails to receive its Second Reading in the Commons, by being talked out by its opponents.

July 1983
In a written parliamentary answer, the Home Secretary, Leon Brittan, announces the establishment of a Committee of Inquiry under Robin Auld, QC, to examine proposals to amend the Shops Acts of 1950–65.

November 1984
The Auld Committee recommends that there should be no legal restrictions on shops' opening hours.

November 1985
The Government's Shops Bill is given its first reading in the House of Lords.

December 1985
Sir Raymond Gower introduces an Early Day Motion calling for MPs to be given a free vote when they debate the Shops Bill. The bill receives its second reading in the House of Lords.

January 1986
The Shops Bill passes through a committee of the whole House (of Lords).

February 1986
The Shops Bill, as amended, passes through the report stage in the House of Lords.

It is given its third reading in the House of Lords and is taken to the Commons, where it receives its first reading.

14 April 1986
The Shops Bill is defeated on its second reading by 296 votes to 282, despite a Government majority of 144 and a Three Line Whip.

Dock Work Bill 1989

Pre-1987
John Townend and a number of other Conservative MPs consistently call for abolition of the National Dock Labour Scheme.

November 1987
Jacques Arnold tables an Early Day Motion calling for repeal of the Dock Labour Scheme. Eventually 228 Conservative MPs sign the motion.

March 1988
During a Consolidated Fund Bill debate, Michael Fallon raises the issue of abolishing the scheme.

May 1988
David Davis proposes a Ten Minute Rule Bill that would, if successful, have required employers and unions to negotiate the repeal of the scheme or face compulsory abolition.

June 1988
The National Association of Port Employees publishes a report suggesting that repeal of the scheme would allow the creation of 50,000 new jobs.

October 1988
Leon Brittan, a former Trade and Industry Secretary, calls for the abolition of the scheme during a fringe meeting at the Conservative Party Conference.

November 1988
David Davis writes *Clearing the Decks*, published by the Centre for Policy Studies, which demonstrates the damaging effects of the scheme.

February 1989
Norman Tebbit, Michael Heseltine, Jacques Arnold, Nicholas Bennet and David Davis are among the sponsors of an Early Day Motion that receives 212 signatures within a fortnight.

March 1989

During Employment Question Time on Budget Day, a group of MPs repeatedly ask the Government to repeal the Dock Labour Scheme.

April 1989

The Government publishes a White Paper on the Dock Labour Scheme. The Dock Work Bill receives its second reading by a majority of 130 and is sent for consideration by a standing committee.

May 1989

Dock Work Bill receives its third reading by a majority of seventy-one and is sent to the Lords.

July 1989

Dock Work Bill receives Royal Assent.

The stages of any campaign are fairly similar:

1 Raise House of Commons and media interest in the issue, by parliamentary and/or extra-parliamentary activity.
2 Win the public argument (which generally means winning the support of the media commentators).
3 Build a winning House of Commons coalition (which means a majority willing to vote for your cause).
4 Win the support of the Government (since controversial legislation cannot survive the Private Member's Bill process).
5 Maintain the coalition by winning the arguments throughout the legislative procedure.

ANATOMY OF CAMPAIGN I

The Sunday trading campaign had started off with a firm bedrock of interest, established over many years by parliamentary activity of various sorts. Although mostly unsuccessful, such activity had the effect of raising public and Government interest in the matter. Thus Mrs Thatcher declared:

The Government accepts that the shops legislation is unsatisfactory and does not correspond to modern patterns of living and can find no ground of principle for opposing changes in present restrictions on shopping hours.

When the last of these bills, Ray Whitney's Private Member's Bill 1983, failed, the Government was finally pushed into setting up a Committee of Inquiry, the Auld Committee. In November 1984 this committee recommended removal of legal restrictions on shopping hours. The main thrust of media coverage was favourable, and opinion polls showed that two-thirds of the public supported the recommendations. Preparations went ahead for a Government bill, and a year later the Shops Bill received its first reading in the House of Lords.

Meanwhile, however, the opponents of reform had mobilized. The Keep Sunday Special movement was an unusual coalition – of the Church, trade unionists and small traders – but it turned out to be formidably effective. By January 1986 the Government had received 16,292 letters against the bill, with only twenty-seven letters of support. Furthermore, the flank of public opinion had been turned. By April an opinion poll showed 70 per cent of the public wanted Sunday working kept to a minimum. A number of large traders, such as Boots and Marks & Spencer, had also indicated a lack of enthusiasm for the idea.

This appearance of change is probably misleading, however. What it reflects is that, while most of those in favour did not feel very strongly about it, many of those against were absolutely vehement. This is why, on specific policies, opinion polls are often viewed by MPs with less interest than their mailbag. It takes no effort to answer a question, but people who write letters generally care a great deal.

That is what happened with the Shops Bill 1986. Numerous people wrote to their MPs or lobbied them in the House. They went to their surgeries. Many Conservative MPs wavered, particularly if they had marginal constituencies. These were influential people who were complaining – their local vicars, small shopkeepers, local trade union leaders. At the end of the day, such influence decided the issue. After its passage through the Lords against the background of a vociferous public campaign, the Shops Bill was defeated on its second reading in the Commons by 296 votes to 282, despite a Three Line Whip. It was one of the greatest upsets in modern parliamentary history, and it was only the third time this century that the Government had been defeated on a second reading.

ANATOMY OF CAMPAIGN 2

Compare this unexpected failure with the success of the Dock Work Bill 1989. By 1987, despite a persistent campaign by a number of Conservative back-benchers (most determinedly by John Townend, the Hull-born Member for Bridlington), the Government still solidly refused to consider reform of the Dock Labour Scheme. The argument against reform was simple. The scheme affected only 10,000 people, down from 80,000 when it was created, and was accordingly 'withering on the vine'. It was not, therefore, worth the risk of a dock strike to eliminate something that was going to disappear of its own accord.

Plenty of Conservative back-benchers disagreed with this view: the November 1987 Early Day Motion, for example, was signed by 228 MPs. There were about 370 Conservative MPs in that session of Parliament; of these about 130 were Members of the Government – ministers, Whips or parliamentary private secretaries – who almost never sign Early Day Motions, thus leaving a theoretical total of 240 available to sign. Allowing for sickness, absence on foreign trips and the fact that some MPs never sign Early Day Motions 'on principle, old chap', 228 was very close to 100 per cent of all possible signatories.

Despite this, and despite a very effective Consolidated Fund Bill debate led by Michael Fallon, the Government refused to budge.

At about this time, another approach was tried. If the strike risk was significant, what about a negotiated end to the scheme? The activists proposed a Ten Minute Rule Bill, designed to create the conditions for a negotiated end to the scheme. As usual, it was defeated, but it established that the Labour Members were not interested in a negotiated end to the scheme, and it gave more publicity to the campaign.

During the summer parliamentary recess of 1988 it was decided to attack the Government's arguments head on, so a paper was written to show that the 'withering on the vine' argument was fallacious. The paper highlighted the way the Dock Scheme destroyed jobs in surrounding areas and pointed out that it could not legally disappear without taking out of operation most of the best ports in the country. It also stressed that, with proper planning, a dock strike was survivable. The paper was published by the Centre for Policy Studies, a very influential political group that had a high reputation with the Whitehall policy formulators. Its publication was timed for the gap between the prorogation of Parliament in November and the Queen's Speech a few days later, since this time was usually short of political news. The tactic was successful. The paper was widely reported and virtually every quality newspaper carried favourable editorials in the following weeks.

According to press reports, the matter went to Cabinet in February. The campaigners had no knowledge of this, however; they had accepted all along that a decision to abolish the scheme would be kept secret until the Government's plans were ready, because of the threat of a strike. So they ploughed on. The guerrilla campaign in Parliament continued, by Early Day Motions, by parliamentary questions and by threats to amend the Employment Bill.

Meanwhile, the campaign was also being fought elsewhere. In the docks, the damage being done by the scheme led to crises in Glasgow, Aberdeen and Grimsby. The parliamentary leaders were spending much of their time commenting on that. Rarely did a week go by without favourable media comment. The Grimsby fish dockers actually asked to be released from the scheme.

Therefore, when abolition of the Dock Labour Scheme was announced, a roar of approval went up from Government Members. The ground had been prepared and adequate support was not in doubt. In the second reading, the debate was fierce, but the Government won by 130 votes – significantly more than its majority. The Social and Liberal Democrats had supported the Government.

The difference from the Shops Bill could not have been more marked – but why? Advocates of reform of Sunday trading were generally quite senior, skilled Members, whilst the driving team behind the Dock Work Bill were essentially new boys, so parliamentary skill should not have been the main factor. However, there were some tactical errors on the Shops Bill; in particular, taking it through the Lords first gave the opponents time to organize and bring serious pressure on MPs before it got to the Commons. With big commercial concerns involved, the Shops Bill supporters should not have been short of resources; the Docks team had virtually none. There was no serious risk to the Government in the Shops Bill; the Dock Work Bill faced the threat of a national dock strike. If one campaign had to fail, superficially it should have been the Dock Work Bill, not the Shops Bill. So why was it the other way round?

The principal difference was in the type of opposition to the bill. Both bills commanded a majority of popular support. The determined opposition to the Dock Work Bill, however, was confined to a small group – the dock workers themselves. Their opposition was clearly that of a vested interest. Over 45,000 letters against the Shops Bill were received by the time of its second reading, so the Shops Bill was lost because of a variant of Lord Hailsham's law about being in the right. Ironically, in view of Lord Hailsham's own opinion on elective dictatorship, the rule can be simply stated as a rule of minority rights. If a sizeable minority of people, spread widely throughout society, feel that a new law is wrong fiercely enough to take political action, then that law is in danger of failure.

13

THE HISTORY AND CONSTITUTIONAL
ROLE OF PARLIAMENT

> 'Power tends to corrupt, and absolute power corrupts absolutely.
> Great men are almost always bad men.' *Lord Acton*

It would be unfortunate to leave this review of Parliament without a brief look at its constitutional role, how it came about and where it is going. Unlike most other Western countries, Britain does not possess a single written document called the 'Constitution'. What it does have is a mixture of documents, procedures, traditions, conventions, laws and institutions that together make up our constitution.

The structure of our constitutional framework, and thereby the form of our political system, has developed gradually. The British constitution is, therefore, best understood by taking a look at historical events surrounding Britain's kings, courts and Parliament.

THE HISTORY OF PARLIAMENT

Until the mid-thirteenth century, the kings of England occasionally summoned their leading peers – their barons and bishops – to their palaces to seek advice. The earliest known use of the term 'parliament' is in an official royal summons to the King's (Henry II) Council, dating from 19 December 1241. Sometimes these gatherings also included commoners chosen by the counties. In 1265 a baron, Simon de Montfort, asked the chief towns as well as the counties each to send two of their leading citizens to the king's palace to discuss matters concerning the country and to voice the opinions of the people in their areas. This meeting was called a 'parliament', the 'speaking place' (from the French *parler*, to speak), and soon became permanently based at the Palace of Westminster. The Parliament now comprised the king, the lords and the commoners. It soon became apparent that the commoners were interested in different matters to the lords. They would therefore move to another room for their own meetings. Once their decisions were made, the full Parliament would meet again and each 'House' – the 'Commons' and the 'Lords' – would report their conclusions to the king.

During the fourteenth century, members of the 'House of Commons' were often punished for criticizing the decisions and actions of the king and his Government. This led to secret meetings where the Commons could vote on their discussions and record the numbers on each side, but not their names. The final outcome became the decision of all of them. During the Commons' discussions a spokesman usually emerged, referred to as the Speaker, and it was he who would report the decisions to the king.

Sir John Guildesborough was Speaker during Richard II's fourth and fifth Parliaments, in 1379 and 1380. He set the important precedent that the Commons had a right to give or refuse approval to planned public expenditure by demanding a statement describing how the supplies were to be appropriated.

This right to approve or deny the monarch's spending was clearly of vital importance. The king or queen therefore tried to make sure that the Members were his or her supporters. Secret debating and voting were stopped. The Speaker had to preside over the debates of the Commons and sum up in the form of a question, on which the House would vote. It was soon clear that it would also be useful for the king to have one of his supporters in the chair; the Speaker would then arrange the business of the House in a way favourable to the king. The Speaker's role was difficult, and some of those who were chosen to do the job really did not want to be elected. There soon developed a struggle between the monarch and Parliament, which came to a head in the Civil War, since when the powers of the monarch have gradually decreased.

The evolution of the House of Commons and the House of Lords, the development of debates and the establishment of the rules that govern the debates have all contributed to the constitution as we know it today. However, there are other controls on Parliament apart from the tradition and history just described.

THE CONSTITUTIONAL ROLE OF PARLIAMENT

Part of Britain's constitution is the framework of laws within which Parliament works. In Britain,* the legal framework is separated into two categories, common and statute law.

COMMON LAW

Common law includes both the Royal Prerogative and judicial decisions. Royal Prerogative refers to the privileges and customary duties of the monarch. It covers, for example, the appointment of ministers, judges and bishops; royal pardons; the dissolution of Parliament; and the declaration of war. Nowadays, these powers are exercised by ministers on behalf of the monarch.

Judicial decisions consist of the precedents laid down by the courts over a long period of time. Such precedents are particularly important when considering civil liberties.

STATUTE LAW

Statute law is law created by Acts of Parliament and is the most extensive and important source of law. Some of the most important constitutional Acts are Habeas Corpus Act 1679; Bill of Rights 1689; Act of Settlement 1701; Acts of Union 1707; Parliament Act 1911; Parliament Act 1949; European Communities Act 1972; European Communities (Amendment) Act 1986 (this implemented the Single European Act 1986).

* Strictly speaking, this relates to England, Wales and Northern Ireland. Scotland's legal framework is different, being based on a Roman style of codified law.

CONSTITUTIONAL CONVENTIONS

Constitutional conventions are fundamental to governing Britain. For example, although the sovereign has the legal right to refuse to give his or her assent to an Act of Parliament, actually to do so would defy convention. Other constitutional conventions include that any bill specifically mentioned in an election manifesto should be given an unopposed second reading in the House of Lords; that the Speaker of the House of Commons is impartial; and that the Prime Minister should sit in the Commons rather than the Lords.

Nearly all written constitutions, such as those of France and America, rely upon conventions, but Britain is unusual because it depends upon conventions to a much larger extent.

The British constitution is flexible and no special procedure is necessary in order to change or amend it – unlike, for example, the American constitution. The statutory aspects of the British constitution can be changed by judicial decisions and statute law, but the conventions change only as habit and behaviour change.

Political authority is based upon the constitution. The British constitution does not recognize the people, except as an electorate that periodically chooses a government. By contrast the American constitution begins with the words 'We, the people . . .' In Britain authority rests not with the people but with the Crown-in-Parliament.

THE CROWN-IN-PARLIAMENT

'The King reigns and does not govern.'   *Adolphe Thiers*

The Crown holds political authority in Britain and this authority is vested in people who hold office on behalf of the Crown. The British Government is Her Majesty's Government and ministers are ministers of the Crown. Parliament meets in the Royal Palace of Westminster and MPs swear an oath to the Crown. The Crown initiates public prosecutions and owns Government agencies, such as Her Majesty's Stationery Office. The Crown does not now exercise political power personally and, in fact, the power of the Crown is dependent upon Parliament in two ways: those who exercise authority on behalf of the Crown must have the confidence of Parliament; and when Crown or Government activities depend upon statute law, the co-operation of both Houses of Parliament is required.

The beginning of every Act of Parliament expresses the concept of the Crown-in-Parliament as follows:

Be it enacted by the Queen's Most Excellent Majesty, by and with the advice and consent of the Lords Spiritual and Temporal, and Commons, in this present Parliament assembled, and by the authority of the same, as follows.

Parliamentary sovereignty is another term for the Crown holding political authority and is defined by common law, not by statute law. Some of the consequences that arise as a result of parliamentary sovereignty are:

- No Parliament can be bound by its predecessors. Each Parliament can therefore legislate exactly as it wishes, and there is no way of giving particular laws any special or 'untouchable' status.
- There is no judicial review of parliamentary decisions in Britain; the courts cannot invalidate any Act of Parliament.
- The United Kingdom of Great Britain and Northern Ireland is a unitary state. It is a multinational community but parliamentary sovereignty is undivided. Parliament can bestow powers to local or regional assemblies but, in the end, Parliament is supreme and can simply abolish any such body, as happened in the cases of Stormont and the Greater London Council. This could not happen in a federal state such as Germany or the USA.

EUROPEAN COMMUNITY

'That silly, sanguine notion ... that one Englishman can beat three Frenchmen encourages, and has sometimes enabled, one Englishman in reality to beat two.' *Lord Chesterfield*, 1694–1773

The constitution has recently become an important political issue. Since the 1970s some of the traditional assumptions about parliamentary sovereignty have been challenged.

   With the European Communities Act 1972, the United Kingdom joined the European Economic Community (EEC), as it was then known. EEC legislation takes precedence over laws passed by the British Parliament when they are in conflict. This did not matter much in practice as long as the British Government could exercise its veto in the Council of Ministers. The passing of the Single European Act 1986 limited the use of this veto, and recently – especially after the European Communities (Amendment) Act 1993 on the Maastricht Treaty – the question of sovereignty has become a serious issue. Lord Chesterfield's dictum, unfortunately, no longer applies.

14

PARLIAMENTARY REFORM

THE POWER OF THE HOUSE

The story is told of a retiring MP and a new boy travelling together on the escalator that connects the Members' car park with the Members' cloakroom. The young Member asked his older and wiser colleague which, of all the possible reforms of Parliament, was the most important or necessary. He thought for a few seconds, before replying that if he had the power to make just one change to Parliament, he would put pin-up pictures of beautiful women along the walls at the sides of the escalator! While this story may be apocryphal, parliamentary reform has always been a constant and controversial issue.

When considering parliamentary reform, it is necessary to remember what the legislative function of Parliament is. The memorandum submitted by the Study of Parliament Group to the House of Commons Select Committee on Procedure during its investigation of 1964–5 summarized the role of Parliament in relation to the executive, as 'influence, not direct power, advice not command, criticism not construction, scrutiny not initiative, and publicity not secrecy'.

REFORMS

THE HOUSE OF COMMONS

There are certain structural reforms of the House of Commons that would go some way towards the more effective use of Parliament. For example, the new select committees have already shown great promise in terms of scrutinizing Government departments, but they could do even more if they were given greater resources in terms of back-up staff. More time could be allocated to debating, on the floor of the House, the reports of the select committees.

Most people today would accept that Parliament cannot be the main agency through which legislation is initiated. This is the proper role of the executive; nevertheless, Parliament should be able to draw up legislation, particularly on subjects of social and moral importance which cut across the lines of party politics. Although some Private Members' legislation is successful, it is not, as we have already seen, very difficult for opponents of a Private Member's Bill to ensure that it fails. Private Members' Bills should therefore be given a better chance of successfully negotiating the legislative process than they are at present.

The party Whips are absolutely necessary for the smooth functioning of Parliament and they ensure that the business of the House can be dealt with efficiently. They are often regarded merely as serving to impose the party leadership's wishes on unwilling back-benchers, forcing them to vote in a way they would not otherwise. The life of an MP would be made very unpleasant, and much more demanding than it already is, if the Whips were not able to arrange the parliamentary business as they presently do. There would be many more late-night, and even all-night, sittings; there would be a breakdown of party unity and loyalty; and there would also be a greater need for all MPs to vote in all divisions, because the Government Whips would not be able to ensure a majority to support its legislation. So the Whips are certainly necessary, as is party loyalty.

On the other hand, MPs are intelligent individuals, and as such they will not necessarily agree with their party leadership on every issue. The Whips should perhaps accept that MPs are occasionally entitled to vote against the party line.

One proposed reform of Parliament is the introduction of some kind of mechanical or electronic voting, rather than Members physically walking through the lobbies. The present system, however, has one very important advantage in that it allows back-benchers to meet their front-benchers during a division. The fact that MPs have physically come to the chamber to vote does emphasize how important voting is in the life of Members.

At present the Speaker's constituents are effectively disenfranchised, in that Speakers cannot represent local interests publicly. One suggested solution to this problem, which was rejected in the House in 1963 by seventy-six votes to sixty-eight, is that Speakers should be given a special constituency called St Stephen's, the electorate of which would be the other MPs. This would mean that the constituents presently disenfranchised would have the opportunity of electing a new MP to represent them. The only possible drawback to this proposal is that, if the House decided not to re-elect a Speaker, he or she would be left without a seat, but this minor hitch is theoretical since the Speaker has always been re-elected, if he or she so wished, ever since 1835.

The 1984 Reform Group survey of MPs suggested that most Members would be in favour of reforming the timetable of the House of Commons. A majority were in favour of the daily proceedings ending at 10 p.m. unless it was decided to continue by a majority vote. However, while late-night sittings seemed to be unpopular, the survey found that a majority of Members were also opposed to the House sitting in the mornings. The problem has been to balance the size of the Commons' workload with the fact that there is a limit to the number of hours every day that Members can reasonably be expected to attend. One reform that is popular among backbenchers is that every bill should have a prearranged timetable so the use of the guillotine would not be necessary.

The Jopling committee was established in 1991 in response to complaints about the procedures of the House, late-night sittings and ineffective use of time. According to the committee's findings, because of the introduction of television and the increase in Members' workload due to the European Community and Northern Ireland legislation, the number of questions and amount of business have increased dramatically in recent years.

The committee's recommendations were implemented in January 1995. They included limiting the use of Friday sittings, introducing Wednesday morning sittings, stricter time limits in debates and earlier notification of recesses. How useful these changes will be in managing the schedule of the House in the long run still remains to be seen, although so far they have proved popular among MPs, not least for curbing the number of late-night sittings that had become so common.

One of the most evident reforms of Parliament since 1911 has been the televising of proceedings. Despite the gloomy predictions, there is no evidence that televising has led to a decline in the standards of behaviour in the chamber or to an increase in the number of frivolous applications for emergency debates. In fact, in many respects it has provided a regulating force.

Another positive aspect of the introduction of television has been a marked increase in public interest in Parliament. One of the results of that has been that expectations and demands on MPs have also increased; the amount of constituency work has risen because of the higher profile of MPs. A result of that extra workload, and of the greater activity in select committees and the like, has been to drive down attendance in the chamber, especially on Fridays, when MPs return to the constituencies to hold surgeries.

THE HOUSE OF LORDS

The House of Lords has been the subject of much criticism over the years, and of several important reforms this century. The main functions of the Lords were described thus by the report of the Conference on the Reform of the Second Chamber, held in 1918:

1 The examination and revision of bills brought from the House of Commons, a function which has become more needed since . . . the House of Commons has been obliged to act under special rules limiting debate.
2 The initiation of bills dealing with subjects of a comparatively non-controversial character which may have an easier passage through the House of Commons if they have been fully discussed and put into a well-considered shape before being submitted to it.
3 The interposition of so much delay (and no more) in the passing of a bill into a law as may be needed to enable the opinion of the nation to be adequately expressed in it. This would be specifically needed as regards bills

which affect the fundamentals of the constitution or introduce new principles of legislation, or which raise issues whereon the opinion of the country may appear to be almost equally divided.

4 Full and free discussion of large and important questions, such as those of foreign policy, at moments when the House of Commons may happen to be so much occupied that it cannot find sufficient time for them. Such discussions may often be all the more useful if conducted in an assembly whose debates and divisions do not involve the fate of the executive government.

The House of Lords is also the highest court in the land, but not all peers participate in this function. Judicial cases are heard by at least three of the Law Lords, who include the Lord Chancellor, ex-Lord Chancellors, the Lords of Appeal in Ordinary, retired Lords of Appeal in Ordinary and members of the Judicial Committee of the Privy Council.

The House of Lords does play an important role in the legislative function and has, in fact, often in recent years been more successful than the Opposition in the Commons in terms of amending and even rejecting legislation. The House of Lords European Communities Select Committee was particularly effective at examining draft European legislation.

Some people are content to make a few structural reforms to the House of Lords; others wish to abolish it outright, especially when the 'other place' (as MPs describe it) crucially interferes with legislation passed by the House of Commons. The House of Lords is a necessary part of British government, but it has, and should have, a subordinate role to that of the – elected – House of Commons. As Lord Hailsham commented, 'The House of Lords exercises influence rather than power.' This is as it should be.

It is for this reason that any suggestion that the House of Lords should be directly elected will fail. If membership of the House of Lords were based on election, it would inevitably come into conflict with the Commons on a much more regular and serious basis than at present.

Parliamentary reform is a difficult issue, and one on which it is unusual to find a broad all-party consensus. The British Parliament has been built up over the years by evolution rather than design. Like the constitution, it is based on interlocking conventions, laws, precedents and procedures. Any reform of any part has knock-on effects on other parts. Many reforms can be made but they must be introduced carefully and, therefore, slowly.

CONSTITUTIONAL REFORM

There has been a great deal of debate about constitutional changes, perhaps because economic hardship has led to discontent with the current British constitutional arrangement. In the 1990s, as in the 1930s and 1970s, there are people who wish to solve cultural problems by constitutional changes. In the 1970s, for example, there was an upsurge of nationalism in Scotland and Wales, and referendums were held on the issue of devolution, which could have changed Britain from a unitary to a federal state. Separate assemblies with devolved powers were then rejected by the Scots and Welsh. In the mid-1990s, however, devolution is back on the agenda. Because of the strength of nationalist feeling, especially in Scotland, the Labour Party has promised that, in government, it would establish a Scottish Parliament in Edinburgh and a Welsh Assembly in Cardiff. Once again, the United Kingdom may become a federal, rather than a unitary, state.

More recently there have been calls for a new written constitution protected by a British Supreme Court and based upon a bill of rights (an Act of Parliament protecting the rights of citizens, such as freedom of speech and freedom of worship). At the moment civil rights in Britain are essentially negative – inhabitants are free to do anything that is not specifically prohibited. Those who call for a bill of rights do so because they fear a future Government might put measures through Parliament that are immune from court review, and a bill of rights would protect the citizen. However, the principle of parliamentary sovereignty means that any Parliament can change any act of a previous

Parliament and it would therefore be impossible to fix a bill of rights permanently. Additionally, parliamentary sovereignty also means that the courts are, in any case, subordinate to Parliament.

Those seeking constitutional reform therefore have to aim for complete change in the constitutional structure, and obviously this is very difficult to do. A new constitution, based on a bill of rights, would bring lawyers into political disputes and take politicians into the courts. There would also be difficulty in deciding what should be included in a bill of rights: freedom of speech and freedom of worship, yes; but what about freedom to strike?

It is quite fashionable to criticize the constitutional state of affairs in Britain today, and phrases such as Lord Hailsham's famous 'elective dictatorship' are commonly bandied around to describe the situation. The reality is, however, that, although our constitutional procedures are a patchwork quilt rather than a seamless robe, they have allowed Britain to avoid the recurrent political paralysis of the United States of America and the totalitarian tyrannies of Stalin's Soviet Union.

The building of our political system has been a long process of practical amendment and refinement and has been relatively continuous since the seventeenth century. In fact, since that century, there has not been a break in the system of government of Britain. At no time have British politicians had to sit down and consider the basic features of the constitution, such as has happened in Germany twice this century, even before re-unification. Ever since the Wilson Government in 1964, as more radical constitutional reconstruction has been demanded, there has been little attempt to co-ordinate these demands, and the actual changes implemented have been only piecemeal.

The debate over constitutional reform is likely to continue for some time and, whatever the outcome, it is valuable in creating an awareness of the British constitution.

By the very nature of the subject, books on the operations of Parliament and Government tend to be either amusing or informative but rarely both. Those listed below, however, bridge this divide to a greater or lesser extent.

GENERAL ASPECTS OF PARLIAMENT AND POLITICS

Austin Mitchell, MP, *Westminster Man* (Thames/Methuen, 1982): a witty, wide-ranging account of how Westminster works from the perspective of a Labour Member of Parliament who has, in his time, been a TV commentator and a teacher of political history.

Richard Needham, MP, *Honourable Member* (Patrick Stephens, 1983): an amusing, easy-to-read account of the career of a fictional MP, from aspiring candidate to junior minister. It gives an insight into how this arcane world looks from the inside.

THE MECHANICS OF PARLIAMENT

Paul Silk and Rhodri Walters, *How Parliament Works* (Longman, 1987): a clear, authoritative work on the rules and procedures of Parliament (both authors are currently clerks: Paul Silk for the Commons and Rhodri Walters in the Lords). A good reference work for those fascinated by the minutiae of what happens in the House.

Philip Norton, *Commons in Perspective* (Martin Robertson, 1981) and (ed.)

Parliament in the 80s (Blackwell, 1985): two books that each give a good overview of how Parliament works, warts and all, by Hull University professor.

THE OPERATION OF GOVERNMENT

Jock Bruce-Gardyne, *Ministers and Mandarins: Inside the Whitehall Village* (Sidgwick and Jackson, 1986): a bitingly witty account of this ex-minister's time at the Treasury. Is full of insights and iconoclasm; a good read that leaves you feeling a great deal wiser.

Gerald Kaufman, MP, *How to be a Minister* (Sidgwick and Jackson, 1980): exactly what it says it is, this refreshingly honest account tells how this Labour front-bencher made his way as a minister. Again full of insights, it should be read by budding politicians!

Peter Hennessy, *Cabinet* (Blackwell, 1986) and *Whitehall* (Secker and Warburg, 1988): Hennessy is the most authoritative Whitehall-watcher among the ranks of journalists. These are both excellent reference works; the first is shorter and an easier read, the second is to go on your reference shelves between the *Encyclopedia Britannica* and the *Oxford English Dictionary*.

AMUSEMENT VALUE

There are many books by parliamentary sketchwriters that simultaneously amuse, communicate the 'atmosphere' and allow an osmotic learning process. Names to look out for are Craig Brown, Simon Hoggart and Edward Pearce, among others. My favourite, however, is Frank Johnson's *Out of Order* (Robson Books, 1982).

INDEX

A SELECTION OF BOOKS FROM BBC/PENGUIN

The Watchdog Guide to Getting a Better Deal
David Berry

Watchdog is probably the most famous and effective consumer-protection programme on television. Although it has inevitably focused on the most dramatic cases and worst abuses, the research team has developed the tools to help ordinary citizens see through the scams and fight back against the sharks. In this invaluable guide to getting a better deal, David Berry gives clear and concise advice on topics such as shopping and what to do about faulty goods, getting good services from public utilities, dealing with hospitals, the police and local authorities, borrowing and investing, holidays and pensions.

The Underworld   Duncan Campbell

From the racetrack gangs and safe-crackers of the 1930s to the hitmen and drug smugglers of today, *The Underworld* is the remarkable story of modern British crime. *Guardian* crime correspondent Duncan Campbell tells of infamous and feared gangsters, unarmed 'gentleman' criminals, the growth in the use of firearms and the role of prisons and borstals in providing the underworld with heroes, and gives accounts of the major players in gun fights, drug rings and clubland carve-ups. Gangland empires, police corruption, shocking headlines and legendary ringleaders all play their part in this gripping and revealing chronicle of crime.

A SELECTION OF BOOKS FROM BBC/PENGUIN

Great Railway Journeys
Photographs by Tom Owen Edmunds

Against all the odds – despite the aeroplane and the motor car – trains are still the best way to travel to discover a country. In *Great Railway Journeys* six travellers write about their railway journeys through terrain for which they have a particular attachment, curiosity and affection.

Mark Tully takes the Khyber Mail from Karachi to the breathtaking Khyber Pass; Clive Anderson explores the route from Hong Kong to Mongolia; Natalia Makarova journeys through her Russian past, from St Petersburg to Tashkent.

Whether by steam or diesel, on cattle trucks, double-decker coaches or the luxury City Gold service, each of these journeys – as well as those undertaken by Lisa St Aubin de Terán, Rian Malan and Michael Palin – turns into an adventure.

Crusades Terry Jones and Alan Ereira

In 1095 Pope Urban II made an announcement that would change the world. He called upon Christians to march under the banner of the Cross and save their brothers in the East from the advance of Islam. This vision of crusading Christianity dominated the events of the next two centuries. With wit and humour, making the history of the Crusades accessible to all readers, Terry Jones and Alan Ereira bring vividly to life the compelling, often horrific, story of the fanatics and fantasists, knights and peasants, corrupt clergy and duplicitous leaders who were caught up in these fervent times.

A SELECTION OF BOOKS FROM BBC/PENGUIN

Plato to NATO
Studies in Political Thought

The question 'Why should I obey the state?' forms the basis of all political philosophy from the time of the earliest civilizations to the present day. It has provoked much debate over the centuries on topics including the definition of liberty, the laws of nature and the intervention of divine power. *Plato to NATO* contains fourteen essays on prominent political thinkers that provide a tantalizing introduction to the works of figures as diverse as St Thomas Aquinas, Hobbes, Machiavelli, Rousseau and Russell. *Plato to NATO* contains an introduction by Brian Redhead, and is ideal reading for students of political history.

Against the State Janet Coleman
Studies in Sedition and Rebellion

In 399 BC the philosopher Socrates was charged and condemned to death by fellow citizens who believed he had acted against the Athenian democracy. In the seventeenth century Cromwell and the regicides chose the same punishment for Charles I. In *Against the State* Professor Janet Coleman looks at the enduring tradition of rebellion against official authority, studying the violent activities of religious martyrs and terrorists, oppositional movements like feminism, and the radical social analyses of Thomas More, Karl Marx and Sigmund Freud. With an incisive introduction by Brian Redhead, *Against the State* is an excellent companion volume to *Plato to NATO*.

A SELECTION OF BOOKS FROM BBC/PENGUIN

Absolutely Fabulous   Jennifer Saunders

Wicked and funny, *Absolutely Fabulous* is the hit television comedy series that blows the lid off the fashion industry. The cast includes PR mogul Edina, slave to every media-induced fad from designer diets to flotation tanks; her alcoholic and sponging best friend Patsy, addicted to everything that's harmful (and probably illegal); and Saffron, Edina's long-suffering, sensible daughter who struggles to stay sane in the midst of the chaos which erupts around her.

A brilliant send-up of all the trends and neuroses that afflict life in the nineties, *Absolutely Fabulous* contains all the episodes from the first series including some scenes and dialogue not eventually transmitted. Written by Jennifer Saunders in her uniquely acerbic style, this book of scripts demonstrates just how fabulous *Absolutely Fabulous* really is!

Absolutely Fabulous 2   Jennifer Saunders

Edina and Patsy, television's most outrageous duo, offer a riotous second helping of the award-winning *Absolutely Fabulous*.

Blazing their way through the world of fashion PR, all their adventures from the second series can be found in this explosive collection of scripts, including the photo-shoot in Marrakesh where Saffy is exchanged for a small amount of dirhams, and disturbing revelations about Patsy in *Hello!* magazine.

A SELECTION OF BOOKS
FROM BBC/PENGUIN

EastEnders: A Celebration   Colin Brake

The full, inside story of the BBC's most popular programme.

No television serial has ever offered viewers as much drama, excitement and gritty realism as *EastEnders*. From its first episode over ten years ago it gripped the nation, and it has kept us enthralled with some of the most compelling storylines and controversial issues – from kidnapping to teenage pregnancies – yet seen on prime-time television. This is the real story – including the tenth anniversary and beyond – of Britain's favourite soap, and it gives the low-down on the who, what, where and when of more than a decade of *EastEnders*.

Casualty: The Inside Story   Hilary Kingsley

Casualty is the BBC's most successful, most gripping medical drama serial ever.

A compelling mixture of soap opera and documentary, it is both hard-hitting and human. Powerful enough to annoy politicians and upset health workers, the inside story of Holby City Hospital's Accident and Emergency Department is always controversial and attracts praise and criticism in almost equal measure. Now you can peek behind the screen and find out all the *Casualty* low-down. Award-winning journalist Hilary Kingsley talks to the creators, the advisers, the cast and crew, gives a resumé of the story, and tells how the make-up and special effects are created and what to expect from the next series. Discover for yourself the true life behind the scenes in *Casualty*.

A SELECTION OF BOOKS FROM BBC/PENGUIN

Island Race   John McCarthy and Sandi Toksvig

As a hostage in Beirut, John McCarthy had a dream of sailing on the bow of a classic yacht: to him it was a powerful vision of freedom. In *Island Race* he teams up with his old friend, comedian Sandi Toksvig, to fulfil the dream by sailing around the coast of Britain. In the beautiful *Hirta*, an eighty-year-old wooden cutter, they call in at nearly fifty ports and harbours, and encounter an enormous range of communities – from Buddhist monks on Holy Island in the north to the busy seaside resorts of England's south coast. In this warm-hearted book, by turns thoughtful and hilarious, the gutsy duo make a great many entertaining discoveries and offer two sometimes conflicting but complementary views of Britain from the sea.

The Making of Pride and Prejudice   Sue Birtwistle and Susie Conklin

Filmed on location in Wiltshire and Derbyshire, *Pride and Prejudice*, with its lavish sets and distinguished cast, was watched and enjoyed by millions. Chronicling eighteen months of work – from the original concept to the first broadcast – *The Making of Pride and Prejudice* brings vividly to life the challenges and triumphs involved in every stage of production of this sumptuous television series.

Follow a typical day's filming, including the wholesale transformation of Lacock village into the minutely detailed setting of Jane Austen's Meryton. Discover how an actor approaches the character, how costumes and wigs are designed, and how the roles of casting directors, researchers, and even experts in period cookery and gardening, contribute to the series. Including many full-colour photographs, interviews and lavish illustrations, *The Making of Pride and Prejudice* is a fascinating insight into all aspects of a major television enterprise.

A SELECTION OF BOOKS FROM BBC/PENGUIN

The Death of Yugoslavia Laura Silber and Allan Little

While the western world stood by, seemingly paralysed, and international peace efforts broke down, the former Yugoslavia was witnessing Europe's bloodiest conflict for half a century. *The Death of Yugoslavia* is the first account to go behind the public face of battle and into the closed worlds of the key players in the war. Laura Silber, Balkans correspondent for the *Financial Times*, and Allan Little, award-winning BBC journalist, plot the road to war and the war itself.

Drawing on eye-witness testimony, scrupulous research and hundreds of interviews, they give unprecedented access to the facts behind the media stories. Could anything have been done to prevent this terrible tragedy? What will be its lasting effects? The authors consider these questions and assess the present situation and its implications for future international relations.

States of Terror Peter Taylor
Democracy and Political Violence

Terrorism is the scourge of most modern democracies, but how can governments fight back without adopting the same terrorist tactics and trampling on those human rights they claim to uphold? In this vivid and disturbing book, based on an acclaimed documentary series, Peter Taylor takes readers inside Irish Cabinet meetings and IRA courts martial. He examines the aims and methods of Palestinian radicals and their Mossad pursuers, and talks to the sons of assassinated enemies who may provide a glimmer of hope. His findings bring fresh insight into one of today's key moral and political issues.

A SELECTION OF BOOKS FROM BBC/PENGUIN

Storm from the East   Robert Marshall

Genghis Khan left an empire more than twice the size of Alexander's; his successors went on to conquer and govern an empire stretching all the way from Korea to the River Danube. Robert Marshall examines the Mongols' breathtaking rise from nomadic herdsmen to world conquerors in just two generations. He describes their devastating invasion of feudal Europe, and Christendom's clumsy attempts to understand these alien invaders, and ends with the empire's decline and fall, after Khublai Khan's triumphant unification of China.

In Search of the Dark Ages   Michael Wood

One thousand years of invasion by Romans, Anglo-Saxons, Vikings and Normans have helped to define the myths, culture and spirit that shape Britain today. Here Michael Wood gives us a vivid portrait of the early kings and conquerors of Europe's oldest kingdom. He charts the facts and legends surrounding the Celtic Queen Boadicea and King Arthur, and the three great Anglo-Saxon kings, Offa, Alfred and Athelstan, and explores the failure of Ethelred the Unready to defend England against renewed Viking invasions, paving the way for the Norman Conquest of 1066.